The Brain Audit

Why Customers Buy (And Why They Don't)

Sean D'Souza

The Brain Audit: Why Customers Buy (And Why They Don't)

Sean D'Souza

Training Programs:
Training. Yes, we do train staff. And we have trained staff. And we do have workshops and we do have online as well as live, in-person workshops.

If you're reading this, and are interested, there's an address below. And a phone number. If you email us, expect to get a response in less than 24 hours. If you don't get a response, it's because your email has been lost somewhere in the great email graveyard. If so, pick up the phone and call.

For information on Psychotactics and The Brain Audit Training Programs, contact:
Online: www.psychotactics.com
Snail Mail: PO Box 36461, Northcote, Auckland 0748, New Zealand.
+64 9 449 0009
+64 21 2361415
Email: sean@psychotactics.com
Secondary: sean@5000bc.com

Published in New Zealand (Where else?)
(Any person flouting these rules will be sent to serve time, picking up sheep poo on some farm in New Zealand)

National Library of New Zealand Cataloguing-in-Publication Data
D'Souza, Sean, 1968-
The brain audit : why customers buy (and why they don't)
Sean D'Souza.
ISBN 978-0-473-17504-7
1. Consumer behavior. 2. Marketing. I. Title.
658.8342—dc 22

Testimonials

"In Jan 2006 we took £3,500 in sales (before The Brain Audit). In Jan 2007 we took £15,000."

"When we set out on our own, we knew we had a great product, and we knew our target audience. But our business was eating money. We were drowning; we could not take a wage.

So I (Debbie) had to do a second job to make ends meet. Our sales were coming in dribs and drabs and the previous year ended in a large loss. We knew nothing about marketing, and just placed ads in magazines and thought customers would come flooding in. How wrong we were!

And then we ran into The Brain Audit and used the principles mentioned in the book. We started with our website and methodically worked our way through every bag on the conveyor belt, not moving onto the next until the one before was done.

As a result, we have halved our advertising costs. Magazines now print our articles and we have customers writing to editors of magazines about us and our products—it's just amazing—the turnaround. We have to pinch ourselves to know that what is happening is real.

To give you an example, in Jan 2006 we took £3,500 in sales (before The Brain Audit). In Jan 2007 we took £15,000 in sales. We now both take a salary, and I have given up my other job, so life is looking real good for us. We ignite classic bikes, and The Brain Audit and Sean have ignited us."

**Debbie Perkins. Partner, Pazon Ignitions,
Tauranga, New Zealand (originally from the UK)**

"Before I purchased The Brain Audit, I thought this is just crazy, I've got so much marketing material that I still haven't implemented."

"But right from Sean's first story and metaphor, I could see this was different. I was hooked. The Brain Audit challenged virtually every principle of marketing I'd grown up with. And it's this refreshing, innovative approach that makes The Brain Audit a "must buy" for anyone who is really serious about challenging the status quo and taking their business to new heights.

Already we've applied the principles to one of our workshops and the response has been fantastic. The Brain Audit and our ongoing association with Sean has been one of the best business decisions we've every made."

Paul Mitchell, Managing Director, The Human Enterprise, Sydney, Australia

"My attendance would sometimes double just by arranging my class flyers using The Brain Audit principles."

"Before The Brain Audit, I used to put on workshops where I would have as many as 45 people show up. Sometimes 10 people. Sometimes I had no one show up. I had no idea how to attract people to the training classes that I offered.

Upon the recommendation of a friend, I learned about The Brain Audit and I decided to buy it. As I began to think like my customers, I would employ the concepts in the marketing for my classes. My attendance would sometimes double just by arranging my class flyers using The Brain Audit principles. I feel much more confident and clear in communicating my value through The Brain Audit."

Gregory Lee, LionHeart Leadership Center, Frederick, Maryland, USA

"I received more response from my direct mail and email advertising than I have in the past."

"Before I bought the Brain Audit, I was wondering how this guy so off the beaten track in New Zealand could possibly know how I could be successful marketing myself in the US. Sean's approach *feels* right on to me. I've decided that it must work if he can sit in NZ and reach into my brain, so successfully, in the US!

For me, the biggest benefit of Sean's work, in addition to understanding how to write copy, was to understand that you can't expect people to buy from you right away. I have applied The Brain Audit to direct mail pieces, and email advertising, and am in the process of overhauling my website. I received more response from my direct mail and email advertising than I have in the past.

I would recommend The Brain Audit, because it lays out a successful approach that I was immediately able to apply, unlike all the other "systems" I've invested in in the past."

Becky DeGrossa, City, Centre For Healthy Divorce, Boulder, Colorado, USA

"My copywriting before The Brain Audit was good, but it was like a tree house."

"I remember sitting down with the freshly printed The Brain Audit in one hand, a hot chocolate with marshmallows in the other, and preparing for a nice reading - but I got way more than that. There are two very specific extra "weapons" that The Brain Audit gave me, that I never got from the many copywriting courses that are out there (and if you're like me, you've got them all, too).

Most courses and books teach you WHAT works. The Brain Audit explains very simply WHY it works, HOW it works. This is master-level applied psychology, necessary for any self-respecting marketer.

The second extra thing that The Brain Audit gave was not just success elements and explanations, but a STRUCTURE. A checklist for the necessary ingredients, a blueprint for your copy. My copywriting before The Brain Audit was good, but it was like a tree house. After The Brain Audit your copywriting will be like a glass and steel superstructure your customers just can't take their eyes off.

I would've liked to cite specific results, but I've been using The Brain Audit for so long I can't keep score any more. I used it in my sales copy for selling manuals, trainings, seminars, memberships or to help my customers sell maps, wine, even electricity.

I'd recommend The Brain Audit to any business owner or marketer who wants to understand the mind of his customer and be able to use this structure, this checklist to write copy more confidently."

Gabor Wolf, Marketing Consultant,
Budapest, Hungary

"I'm not a psychologist. I'm an engineer."

"I used The Brain Audit on my website (which is unfortunately only for German speaking people). And all The Brain Audit principles are still not implemented in the correct way (A new revision is on the way). But what's interesting is the use of especially the first three red bags in my consulting work, e.g. with start-up companies or during my work as a quality management representative and trainer. To see how the brains of people begin to work when they think about the questions, and to hear the quality of the answers, is really amazing.

I recommend The Brain Audit to people to clarify the focus of their work, because it is a simple and sound step-by-step system easy to implement."

Dr. Richard Schieferdecker, Consultant/Trainer,
Aachen, Germany.

Dedication

I really should dedicate this book to my wife, Renuka, but for whom doing anything around Psychotactics would be close to impossible. Or perhaps I should dedicate it to my parents, Winnie and Edmund, who gave me infinite freedom to read, write and draw. Without the solid grounding they gave me, my life would have been a lot tougher.

And then again, this book would never have seen the light of day, if I hadn't read *Good to Great* by Jim Collins. That book made me drop a flourishing cartooning career to go into an even more satisfying career in marketing.

So as you can see, dedicating the book to one entity is going to be more than a little tough. But hey, I do have someone in mind.

I really, really, really want to dedicate this book to that customer who asked me for notes. You see, The Brain Audit wasn't really a book. It was just a speech I gave. And after I gave the speech way back in the year 2002, I walked away after the applause—as you do.

Well, this person in the audience wanted notes. Sure, she'd scribbled furiously during the presentation itself. But could I, perhaps, give her notes as well? I was aghast at the thought of having to write those notes, but I did. And those notes became our first e-book. That e-book formed the bedrock of the Psychotactics business and has generated tens of thousands of customers, not to speak of dollars.

Those notes formed the launching pad for Brain Audit speeches, training programs, two-three day courses, audio, video, website, blog, and yes, this book itself. Those notes have helped build strategic alliances, clients and friends across the world. Yes, those notes have gone from a skinny 16 pages to a chunky 150 odd pages, but it all started with those notes.

So I guess I'll dedicate this book to that person who asked for the notes. Thank you. Thank you. Thank you.

Whoever you are ☺

Contents

Blatant Praise

Every time I leave an airport, I remember Sean D'Souza.

And if you're a return visitor to the powerful little 'conveyor belt' metaphor that kicks off The Brain Audit, you know exactly what I mean.

And if you're not, you're about to find out.

The 'conveyor belt' metaphor sticks of course, because it works. And because it's an original, just like so many of the other tools that Sean uses to teach. And it's why I believe you'll get so much out of 'The Brain Audit'.

Sean can't say what I'm about to say, because he's too humble. But after a few years of reading his stuff, I've come to a conclusion. Sean is a master of pointed, heaven-sent metaphors and stories.

I don't know if this ability to write metaphorically stems from his background with the Leo Burnett Advertising Agency; or because he comes from a long family of professional teachers. What I do know is that you're going to enjoy the experience that lies ahead in this book.

I should, in an introduction to a book, tell you more about the book itself.

But honestly, I'd rather let Sean do that.

Instead, I'll spend my couple of inches of ink telling you a little more about Sean, if you don't mind. For instance, you might not know Sean is 'that guy.' You know the kind. He's the guy who actually does get up every morning at 4 am And then oozes energy all day long. When I first met Sean, it was via email—with a torrent of ideas of how to increase my income—unsolicited. Just because he liked what I was doing.

His generosity is astounding. To tell you the truth, I doubt he could have held back even if he wanted to. I think you'll find that he's been just as generous in this book. The Brain Audit isn't long, and yet the ideas are densely packed. No fluff, no fake analysis just to fill the pages or appear fancy, just unvarnished marketing truth. And the core of customer psychology as only Sean could draw it into plain view.

People halfway around the world are already talking and using Sean's principles to boost their business success. And as this book gets into more hands, the conversation around these ideas is only likely to increase.

Read on, even if you've read this before. I think you'll see what I mean. And then when you're done, read this book again. There's that much to absorb.

And that's my official directive to you.

Even after sixteen years of working in the writing field on my own, I've learned plenty from Sean. And I learn more with every additional reading.

I'm certain you will too.

John Forde
Paris, France

Too Busy?

Writers often forget that readers are busy.

Readers have little time to go through three hundred pages of material. When faced with daunting prose, readers put it aside, never to see it again.

This information is too important to put aside.
Therefore I have kept this book as concise as possible. And to make sure you absorb the information, you'll find this book is peppered with cartoons. And summaries. And checklists. And then some more cartoons.

These aren't space fillers.
They're learning tools. The brain struggles with new information, or even information put in a new way. That's because the brain is trying so very hard to understand the concepts, and at the same time, put the concepts into some practical application. The cartoons, checklists and summaries are tools that help you not only refresh your learning, but give you multiple layers as well. And they help the brain absorb the information more efficiently.

As you're reading this book, you'll run into concepts that you'll be able to apply right away. And you'd do well to make notes, or mind maps as you go along, so you quickly assimilate the information. If you're reading the book for the second or third time, it would help to have your website, brochure, email or any business communication ready while you read it. It will help you audit the communication as you go along. It will make the experience more interactive. And more effective.

And finally ...
As simple as the concepts are, I would recommend you read this book no less than three times. Why? Simply because each reading

will bring a new understanding which can then be applied with far greater potency.

You may think I'm joking. Surely one reading is enough, you'd think. Who has the time to read a book three times over, you wonder? Well, it's a recommendation. Read it again. And again. And again. And find out for yourself.

However there's one little thing before we get cracking.
This isn't the first version of The Brain Audit. So if you've read this book before, you'll want to know what's new. And this brief section is meant to specifically drive you to concepts that are important, but weren't in earlier versions.

Therefore, if you've read the book before[1], I'd recommend you first go to the newly added concepts and read them in great detail. When you've read them a couple of times, then read the entire book from start to finish.

This technique of isolating the sections and then reading the entire book may seem tedious, but in fact it's very efficient. You'll remember the concepts better than before, and you'll instantly spot where you're going wrong with your current sales letters, your website, etc. In short, you'll become a better auditor than ever before. Okay, time to isolate the new stuff!

How to Isolate the Problem (pages 16-20):
In earlier versions, we talked about the importance of the 'Problem.' And while it's important to recognise the power of the 'Problem,' it's also important to recognise that if you bring up too many problems in your message, you not only scare off the customer, but you're also unable to drive home the importance of the problem in all its detail.

---

[1] If you're reading this book for the first time, I'd recommend reading the entire book from end to end to get the essence of the concepts. Once you've finished reading the book at least twice (or thrice as recommended), make sure you return to this page, and then focus on the specific 'What's New' sections mentioned above.

Process vs. Solution (page 28):
In some instances, we tend to confuse our process with the 'Solution.' What's the difference between the process we follow and the 'Solution'? You'll find the explanation on Page 28.

Target Profile (pages 36-57):
This may seem like the ol' Target Audience chapter, and it's not. It's different. And not just different for the sake of being different. This 'Target Profile' not only reduces your workload tremendously, but it also increases the emotion and power in your message. Read this chapter. Read it well. Read it often. Easily the most important chapter in the book.

The Roller Coaster Effect (pages 63-65):
Often we bring up the 'Problem' and then promptly drop it. This isn't a good idea. The 'Roller Coaster Effect' goes into a little detail about why you need to drive home the problem.

The Wife/Husband/Accountant/Business-Partner Test (pages 75-78):
Starting with the last paragraph on page 75, you'll run into the real reason why you need to create a list of objections. Continue reading onwards to page 78 to figure out how to create a comprehensive list of objections.

The Six Questions For An Outstanding Testimonial: (pages 89-90):
Remember how the earlier versions of The Brain Audit introduced you to these six questions? Well, there's a slight variation in the questions so you can get more precise answers. There's also the reasoning behind why each of the questions is being asked. And why it's imperative to ask all six questions.

The Link Between Testimonials and Objections (pages 91-93):
You may not have realised it before (and I sure didn't), but there's an umbilical cord between testimonials and objections. Find out how they're related, and why the relationship is critical, especially as the customer is very close to making a decision at this point. This link

reduces the resistance the customer feels, so understanding this relationship is pretty darned important if you ask me.

The Hidden Risk (pages 102-105):
There's always a hidden risk involved in any transaction. Obviously, this isn't your standard 100% money-back guarantee. So what's the hidden risk? Start with the last paragraph on page 102, and then keep reading till page 105.

Naming the Guarantee (page 106):
Hmmm, most of us never name our guarantee/warranty. Find out why it's important. And yes, there are examples too.

Butter Chicken Recipe (pages 113-114):
No, you're not seeing things. It's a recipe for butter chicken. And if you want to impress the heck out of someone, follow the instructions.

How To Create Uniqueness-The Steps: (pages 129-136):
In a way the entire chapter has been approached from a different perspective, so reading the entire chapter with a fresh mind will help. However, if you want to cut to the chase, then pages 129-136 will help you, um, cut to the chase.

Checklists (pages 140-148):
Yup, this is new. And there's space in the book itself if you want to write in the book. I can't bring myself to write in books, and if you're like me you may want to go online to www.brainaudit.com/checklists to get a downloadable set of copies.

Hmmm, that's a fair chunk of new stuff. And now it's all isolated, so you can go directly to the new stuff, or at least know how to find it quickly. Don't blame me if you end up reading the book over and over again, anyway. ☺

No Entiendo

Imagine I offered you the vacation of a lifetime.

Imagine you were able to fly first-class to any place on the planet. For three weeks you and a friend could stay at the best hotels; devour the most exquisite cuisine; even get a credit card with no spending limit. And yes, the offer would have no catch. You wouldn't have to buy any thing, or even be grateful to anyone in particular.

Would you turn down the offer?
Despite the irresistible nature of the offer, I'd say that most people would not take up the offer. Notice I didn't say: 'Turn down the offer'. I said: 'They wouldn't take up the offer'. And there's a reason why the most irresistible offer gets little or no response at all.

You see I made the offer in a foreign language.
The offer was made in a language unknown to you. Naturally you would not understand a word I said. And so it is with your audience. You may make the most bewitching offer in the world, and all you're likely to get is a confused look from your audience.

And the reason for the confusion or lack of excitement on the audience's part, is simply because you're speaking in a foreign language. And the same concept of language applies to your customer's brain.

Your customer's brain is attracted to one language.
Yet you're selling or marketing your product or service in quite a different language. Yeah, we all know how mesmerising your offer is—but hey, results are elusive until you speak in a language your customer understands well.

Which means that you get an instant response the moment you switch to the customer's language. Your customer nods. He smiles.

He shakes your hand vigorously. And yes, he wants to sign-up right away. Amazing as it may seem, the offer hasn't changed. But the language—ah, that's changed for sure!

The Brain Audit is a language the brain understands.
It's not a language of persuasion. Or coercion. It's doesn't psyche the customer into buying against his or her will. It's simply a language the brain understands and responds to. And the reason why the brain is so prompt with the response will become crystal clear, as you learn how to present the information in a sequence.

But surely brains don't think sequentially, you think.
Well they do. Your brain uses a sequence, and so does your customer's brain. We just do the sequencing so darned quickly that we fail to see the steps. The Brain Audit freeze-frames the steps so you can see each step. And literally know what the customer is thinking of next. And next.

In fact, the moment you've finished reading a few chapters, you'll be laughing nervously. You'll realise that The Brain Audit can instantly put a lot of 'oomph' into your communication. And yet, you'll feel a little uncomfortable.

Because even as the 'aha-factor' kicks in, you'll begin to realise that you're going to have to make some changes in your presentations; your business cards; your brochures; your website, etc.

And you'll gulp silently.
But don't let the gulp bother you. Because the good news is that even though you'll have to re-do some of your marketing and sales communication, you'll now step up to becoming an auditor.

An auditor who has a set of benchmarks.

Because if you were to ask someone to critique your business cards, they'll simply give you an opinion. But the opinion will be inconsistent from person to person.

But as a Brain Auditor, you're going to have consistent benchmarks.
The reason why you'll get consistent results with The Brain Audit, is because you're not going to base your communication on the '*iffiness*' factor. You're actually going to follow a simple structure.

And the best way to use the structure of The Brain Audit is to use the concepts as an auditor would. So just as an auditor looks at something after it's complete, you too should do the same. Create your web page, and then audit it. Create a presentation first, then go clean it up. Create an advertisement, and only then fix the glitches.

Audit your communication a lot, and you'll slowly pick up the grammar of The Brain Audit. You'll steadily pick up the words. And before you know it, you'll master the language.

It's a language that we use every single day at Psychotactics.com.
We use the language of The Brain Audit to help us sell our products and services. And thousands of clients from countries all over the world have used it to get results both for themselves, as well as for their own clients.[1]

Which brings us back to the vacation of a lifetime.
Use the concepts of The Brain Audit; add a dose of hard work, and you'll be able to write your own ticket to not just one, but many vacations. Now this book isn't a magic potion. But it gives you a deep insight into what makes our brains respond, and what causes our brains to ignore a message. The *ickiest* feeling in sales and marketing is one when you've got a great product or service and the audience just won't respond.

This book is dedicated to erasing that *icky* feeling forever.

---

[1] Hungary, Australia, India, France, Italy, Canada, United States, United Kingdom, Thailand, ... (You're getting the idea, aren't you?)

Warm regards from the land of 44 million sheep (give or take a few million)

Sean D'Souza
Auckland, New Zealand

P.S.: No hurry, but when you put down this book, you'll also find some goodies at www.brainaudit.com. Go there, for updated information, audio and video.

P.P.S.: I know you're keen to start this book on page one. Well here's a tip. Go to page 89 instead. And here's what you'll find. You'll find six questions you can ask your customers. When you ask these six questions, you'll get a testimonial that's detailed and a mile long. You can literally jump right to page 89; read the page; put down the book and call a customer.

And see instant results before the hour is through.
Try it. You'll be very pleased with the results.

The Brain Audit

Understanding why customers do the cha-cha-cha

Is the Brain a 'Conveyor Belt'?

Is the brain predictable? Or is it random? Is it male or female? This little introduction will give you a slightly different insight into how the brain processes information. It will show you why a customer decides to buy, or to forego the purchase.

Best of all, when you are selling your product or service, you can actually identify at which point you forgot to take a 'bag' off the conveyor belt. And why this action causes the customer to back away, just as they're about to sign on the dotted line.

But what's this conveyor belt all about?

The brain works just like a conveyor belt.
Imagine you just got off a long flight, and you're waiting for your

bags to come out on the conveyor belt.[1] When you got on the flight, you loaded seven red bags onto the plane.

As you wait with the other passengers, you see one red bag, and then two. Then three, until you seem to have just six red bags.

So when do you leave the airport?
The question is academic and almost pointless. Without doubt, you leave when you have every one of your seven red bags.

If you don't take all the 'bags' off the customer's brain, the 'bags' go round and round, causing the customer to put off the purchase.

---

[1] You say 'carousel'; I say 'conveyor belt'. As long as we know what we're talking about, we're okay.

No matter how late you are or how tired you felt, you wouldn't leave without every one of your seven red bags.

Customers behave in exactly the same manner.
Customers have this conveyor belt going around in their brains. And when you fail to take out even one of the bags, customers wait for you to give them all the reasons to buy. If you leave even one bag out of your pitch, your customers tend to avoid making a decision.

In fact, it's a good idea to watch customers.
Do you notice how they get a little edgy? Have you seen how they mull over paperwork? How they say they'd 'like to think about it'? Fidget, fidget, fidget, they go. Then it's 'mumble-something-under-their-breath'-time. And you never see those customers again.

The truth is, it isn't hard to get and keep the attention of a customer all the way to the sale—and beyond. But time after time, we let customers walk away and lose the sale. Losing a sale is bad enough. Not knowing which 'red bag' caused you to lose the sale, will drive you even more crazy. If you knew exactly which factor was missing, you could fix it. And never lose the customer again.

This is where we get off the menacing randomness of the conveyor belt and get into the realm of structure. The structure of identifying each of the seven bags, and then systematically removing each bag off the conveyor belt, so that the customer can understand just what you're selling and why they should buy it right away.

Before we go ahead, let's take a good look at what the red bags are; how they play a role in getting a customer's attention; keeping that attention; and then how all these steps end up getting you the sale.

Voila! The whole set of red bags:[2]
Bag No. 1: The Problem
Bag No. 2: The Solution
Bag No. 3: The Target Profile
The Trigger
Bag No. 4: The Objections
Bag No. 5: The Testimonials
Bag No. 6: The Risk Reversal
Bag No. 7: The Uniqueness

[2] When I speak at a 45-minute to one-hour engagement, I often cover the first three bags of The Brain Audit. Invariably, someone in the audience—whose curiosity is aroused— will ask me to give them the entire list of seven bags. They dutifully jot down what I've said and they walk away content in the knowledge that they now know all the seven bags.

But as you can tell, it's not enough to just have a list of the bags. What's really important is the specifics of each bag, and then how it ties together to form a complete message. But even as I write this, I know there are some audience members with a wonderful list of seven red bags, and with zero ability to implement the information into their marketing and sales. That's why I wrote this book. So they can read about— and more importantly— implement the information by understanding the application of each of the bags in detail.

The Problem

Why problems attract customers

Bag 1: The Problem

Imagine you're driving down the highway. You don't seem to have a care in the world. You're listening to the music, you're watching other cars as you pass them by. And you're mildly aware of the quickly changing scenery as you whizz down the road.

And then, from the corner of your eye, you notice something. You notice some red and blue flashing lights. What do you do? Almost instantly your foot goes on to the brakes. No matter what your speed, you seem overly eager to slow down.

So what caused you to quickly change your speed, and get instantly alert? You know the answer as well as I do. It was the red and blue flashing lights of the police car ahead, that caused your brain to do some pretty smart calculations. And that in turn caused you to slow down.

So why did the brain act in this manner?
The brain recognises a problem long before it recognises the solution to the problem. In a millisecond, the brain was able to work out the ramifications of what would happen should the policeman decide to focus on you. In those fractional seconds, the brain worked out how your trip would inevitably be delayed, and how you could cop a fine— among other nasty problems.

Your brain is trying to keep you alive for obvious reasons.

Your brain is indeed obsessed with problems. And for good reason too. The brain's job is to keep you alive, and yes, to help you reproduce and advance your species (In this book, we'll be concentrating on how your 'brain keeps you alive'.)

And to keep you alive, your brain starts to catalogue all the things, events, situations and experiences it needs. And very quickly it works out what's an irritant, what's kinda dangerous, and what's really scary. Which means that if I were to throw a tiny piece of cloth your way, you'd probably raise an eyebrow. But if I threw a block of wood instead, you'd be ducking, swerving and defending yourself in the best way possible.

That's your brain at work. And that smart little brain does one heck of a lot in a matter of milliseconds.

Brain sees change   Brain recognises severity of problem   Brain saves your butt

In any given situation your brain goes through these quick steps:
Step 1: Your brain sees change
Step 2: It recognises if you're going to be in trouble—or not
Step 3: It takes measures to get out of the way.

Which is why you tend not to step in dog poo.
Logically, dog poo should be the last thing on your mind as you walk down the street. Because as you look around you on the street, there are wonderful things to see. Stores full of goodies; restaurants filled with customers and enticing menus; interesting looking men, women and children passing you as you saunter by.

And then your brain sees it.
Right in front of you, in the midst of your wonderful surroundings, is dog poo on the pavement. And all the great goodies, restaurants, people and things go out of focus, as the brain takes every possible step to make sure you don't step in the poo.

Poo is icky. Poo is sticky. Poo has caused you enough trouble in the past. So while it's nowhere as life-threatening as the block of wood, your brain knows that it needs to focus on poo. As you can clearly see, the problem has got your attention to the exclusion of everything else.

'Poo' isn't a big problem, but it's a problem all the same. A problem you'd take pains to go around.

Just like the problem gets Lisa's attention.
Let's take the example of Lisa. Lisa's laptop isn't quite working as efficiently as it should. But it's not a big worry for Lisa–not yet. Then as she's walking down the street, Lisa sees a sign that says: 'Is your laptop acting weird? It could be the first signs of an imminent hard disk crash'.

Suddenly, the sign has elevated Lisa's minor irritation into a bit of a crisis. Lisa can picture her laptop die right in the middle of an important presentation. She can see the computer crash after she's put in a full day's work.

That computer problem which was just an irritant, is now recklessly racing to the top of her to-do list.

As you can see, problems seem to activate our brains.
And when you bring up the problem in your marketing materials, sales pitches and presentations, you are in turn activating the brains of your customers.

But how can we be so sure?
How can we be positive that the problem generates more brain activity than a solution? Let's look at the research. Let's look at the tests done by John Cacioppo, Ph.D., at Ohio State University. [3]

John Cacioppo showed a bunch of people three sets of pictures. The first set normally arouses positive feelings (say, a Ferrari or a pizza). The second set of pictures stir up a problem in your brain (a mutilated face or dead cat). And the third set of pictures produce neutral feelings (a plate, a hair dryer).

Dead cats get more attention than gleaming red Ferraris. How come? Well, that's just how our brains work.

And of course, as researchers tend to do, he faithfully recorded electrical activity of each participant's cerebral cortex. The cerebral cortex in turn, reflects the magnitude of information processing taking place.

The brain—Cacioppo demonstrated—reacts more strongly to stimuli it deems problematic. Or to put it another way, when faced with a problem vs. a solution, the problem really gets our attention.

As you can imagine, the neutral objects didn't excite the brain at all. Plates and hair dryers were deemed too boring to get our brains all excited. But what was surprising during the research finding, was that our brains were more aroused by a problem than a solution.

You'd think a gleaming red Ferrari would have really got the pulse racing—and it did.

But when shown images of problems, the brain activity stepped up to a much higher degree.

[3] Referenced from Psychology Today: 20 June 2003

So yes, problems get our attention, better than anything else.
Yet, most of us don't communicate with problems. Instead we
bring up solutions. And there's a specific reason why we bring up
solutions. Most marketing or sales courses have completely side-
stepped the importance of the problem. Most courses or books will
tell you to highlight the benefits of a product or service.

And what are benefits, but solutions?
So while the brain is focused on the problem, we use the solution/
benefits to get the attention of our customers. Is it any wonder that
your marketing and sales doesn't get the kind of response you're
expecting?

But waitasec, aren't problems a negative way of looking at things?
And are we just making up problems to scare customers?

Are we?

**Let's put this doubt to rest with an
example.**
You're doing fine driving your 1980s
sedan. It has a few dents and looks a
little dated, but you don't care. Until
you have to start showing up for
corporate meetings where everyone
else owns a flashy car. Suddenly
what seemed like a reasonable form
of transport has become a bit of an
embarrassment. The problem wasn't
top of mind a few weeks ago, yet
suddenly you're acutely aware of how
much you need to get a more 'socially-
acceptable' car.

Your dented car doesn't embarrass
you until you start going to corporate
meetings. Then suddenly you're pretty
darned sure that your current car
needs to be replaced—with one that
befits your new found status.

Suddenly you have a problem that didn't exist a while ago.

Suddenly you're a lot like the passenger in Economy Class of every airline.

A passenger in Economy Class only has a problem because they're aware of the splendour of Business Class or First Class. If business or first class didn't exist, not one of us would refer to economy class as 'cattle class'.

By creating Business Class and First Class, airlines created a problem that just didn't exist.

It's the same story with computers. Remember the 486? Okay, so you don't. But in the good ol' days when 486's were the fastest computer, everyone dreamed of moving from their clunky 386 to the wonderful 486. Then the Pentium processor came along, and the 486 became too slow and almost unbearable. Of course, computer processors change all the time, and faster, sleeker processors take their place.

Chug-chug computers. Chug-chug software. Chug-chug cars. Eventually all new and improved products and services are based on solving a chug-chug problem.

A fast processor that seems to be a solution today, is a problem tomorrow. A new car that's shiny and wonderful today, is a problem tomorrow. And so it goes: whatever you're selling only has add-on value if you're solving a problem. If you're not solving a problem in some new and interesting way, then what's the point of your product or service?

This affirms that we're not making up problems to scare customers into buying our products/services. All we're really doing is highlighting the issues that exist. And showing customers how their lives can be better, if they adopt our products/services. And of course, we do this by highlighting the problem.

Which in itself brings up a big issue: problems seem to be a negative way to communicate. Won't this negative attitude turn off the customer?

Are We Being Too Negative?

It's a valid question.
And there's a valid answer.
You're not being negative at all. Highlighting a 'problem' is no different than your telling a child to look both ways before crossing the road. Or telling a friend to make sure they don't see a specific movie, because the story line is plainly boring.

Instead of being a scaremonger, the problem is an educational tool.
It brings to the fore factors that already exist. What's more, a problem may reveal a situation that you aren't currently aware of.
A situation that could get you in trouble if you're not careful.

Like for instance, if your cam-belt[4] breaks on the highway.
What's a 'cam-belt' you ask? Well, I didn't know either, 'til the mechanic looked at my odometer on the car dashboard. "You've done well over 100,000 km", he said. "And you need to make sure your cam-belt is fixed".

And notice what's happening? While the mechanic is giving me these dire warnings I've begun to realise something quite interesting: the cam-belt isn't even broken.

You're advised by the Weather Bureau to take an umbrella, because it's going to rain. Is the Weather Bureau being negative by issuing the rain warning?

But ah, what happens if the cam-belt does break?
The engine starts alright, but the engine would turn over without any compression at all. Once the darned cam-belt breaks, your car's

---

[4] Called 'timing belt' or 'timing chain' in some parts of the world.

engine starts without compression, causing the valves to bend. Once that happens you're in big trouble. Trouble that will cost you a mini-fortune.

But hey, my cam-belt wasn't broken. It didn't even seem frayed. The car ran just fine. In fact, the car had done over 175,000 km (that's 75,000 more than the cam-belt should have been exposed to).

But the problem remains. One day, the cam-belt will break. And do I want to wait for that day? Do I really want to spend mucho dollars? From a total state of ignorance, I've gone to being a bit of an expert on cam-belts.

The problem exists.
You aren't making it up.
You aren't being negative.

You are actually educating your audience, which isn't aware of the problem until you bring it up. Even if your customers weren't thinking about cam-belts (or whatever it is you're selling) ten minutes ago, that product/service now becomes a must-have item. In effect, all you're doing is creating a factor of urgency; elevating a problem to code-red.

Your customer is juggling several problems all at once. If you don't elevate the problem, your customer will never notice your product or service.

Elevating a problem ensures that your product or service gets higher priority than everything else.

So how do you elevate the problem?
You've got to recognise that your customer already has squillions of things to worry about.

Things like picking up the kids from school. Like that board meeting later in the day. Like that new software that's giving him a headache. And while your customer is dealing with all of those day-to-day headaches, that very same customer is dealing with peripheral problems like not stepping into poo, and avoiding flying blocks of wood.

Amidst all this clutter of problems, we have to get the customer's attention. And we have to do so in a way that the customer will at least show some interest in the product/service we have to offer.

But how do you get the customer's attention amidst all this chaos?

You isolate the problem.
Every product or service solves several problems simultaneously. So if you look at a mug of coffee, it solves various problems. For some, that mug represents a break from work. For some, it's a way to meet a friend. For some, it's a business meeting. And for others, it's just a pick-me-up after a tiring session.

The problem arises when we try to send out your problem-based message to all of the above groups. More often than not, we'll want to get all our customers with the least amount of effort, and so we'll take the route that is bound to meet with failure. We'll create a problem-based message that appeals to everyone.

Instead, what we should be doing, is isolating the problem.

How to Isolate the Problem

So let's take an example of problem isolation.
Let's imagine you went to the doctor and said, "I'm not feeling well". What would the doctor say next? He'd ask you to describe what you were feeling. And you'd tell him you were getting persistent headaches.

You see what you've just done? You could have simply said you were not feeling well. And the doctor would be stumped. He'd have to ask more questions. And if you insisted on feeling unwell, without describing the symptoms, he'd have to resort to a battery of tests, to diagnose if there was indeed something wrong with you.

But if all the tests came back without any trace of a problem, the doctor would be unable to help in any way. For the doctor to be of some help, you'd either have to be able to pinpoint a problem, or the tests would have to isolate something that could be the problem.

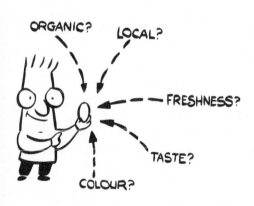

The same principle of isolation applies when you're selling to a prospective customer. If your product or service doesn't isolate a problem, then the customer can't relate to what you're selling.

But on the other hand if you isolate the problem, the customer is quickly able to lock in to the problem, and then investigate what kind of solution you're bringing to the table.

What problem are you solving when you sell an egg? Every product or service solves many problems. To get your message out effectively, you have to isolate the problem. In other words, choose ONE.

So let's take two business examples.

Example 1: Website strategy workshop.
Let's say you were about to conduct a website strategy workshop,
how would you go about isolating the problem?

It's not hard to identify the problem. In fact, within a short time, you
can draw up a list of issues that any website owner would want to
solve. And let's say you compiled a big list and then whittled it down
to about four problems.

The four problems:
1) Attracting clients
2) Getting clients to buy a
   product/service
3) Getting clients to come back to
   buy repeatedly
4) Selling without being a 'snake-
   oil pedlar'.

Of course, if you're selling a course,
your course may deal with all of the
above problems. But trying to get all
these messages across is a bit futile.
Because even one problem, when
properly dealt with, will attract a swarm of customers.

Isolating the problem means specifically
speaking to customers that have 'cat
allergies' vs. 'allergies'. The isolation
allows the customer to 'lock in' to what
you have to say.

So let's say you isolated the fear of how to be profitable online
without becoming a 'snake-oil pedlar'. Now you can write or send
out a message that directly gets the attention of the customer. And
the message runs like this:

Are you sick and tired of internet systems that force you to become a
'monster'? (Most internet training systems 'convince' you to do things
that you think are yucky. They make you believe that the only way to
get sales, is to use methods that border on 'sleazy behaviour.' So is there
a way to be ethical and still bring in growing amounts of revenue?)

You see how an isolated problem created a powerful case for the workshop? In this specific case, we're only speaking to those who feel that the methods used online are 'yucky'. We only want to speak to those who feel the need to run a profitable, yet ethical internet business.

And so we're isolating just one problem.

Sounds scary? Yes, it is indeed scary. But it also gets your attention better than any other method, as you're about to find out in the example to follow.

Example 2: An allergy clinic.
Let's say you run a service where you treat allergies. And it's plain that allergies are a big problem. So what do you do to get your customer's attention?

You simply run ads that say: 'Got Allergies? We'll get rid of them for you.' And admittedly, a headline like that will still get attention, but will it get the attention it deserves? Your advertising and marketing is screaming 'get rid of allergies', without isolating the problem.

And if we were to isolate the problem, we'd have a list.
For example:
1) Pollen allergies
2) Sugar-based allergies
3) Dust allergies.

And of course, you'd protest. You'd say that your allergy clinic can solve all of the above, so why not simply say 'we eliminate all allergies' instead of isolating each and every type of allergy separately?

Yes indeed, you can detect and fix allergies that range from glutamates, salicylates, grasses, mould, dogs, cats, fungus, and yada, yada, yada.

But we're isolating each category. So if we were to go about isolating pollen allergies, we'd talk just about pollen. And we'd bring up issues only related to pollen. When we isolate the problem, we're able to talk only about pollen, and every single one of those customers who want to eliminate pollen allergies, will make a beeline to your door.

But what if you don't know that you have a pollen allergy?
What then? Because it's possible that you don't know what you're allergic to. Wouldn't an ad that talks solely about allergies work better?

Not really.

Because even if your customers aren't aware of what's causing the allergy, they're still able to detect when the allergy is affecting them: e.g. change of seasons; when they go to bed; have a glass of wine.

And therefore the message that gets the customer's attention would read like this:
Do you find you sneeze a lot just before you go to bed?
Do you find you sneeze a lot after a glass of wine?

So we're still isolating. Maybe we're not isolating the type of allergy, but the time or season that triggers the allergy. And instantly our brains recognise that time of day, change in season, or specific activity we are isolating. And the advertisement gets our attention.

This isolation of the problem is necessary because people are busy. They're busy with their problems. And unless the problem you state is crystal clear, they may be more than likely to miss your message.

But if you run an allergy clinic, you'll still be protesting. And the protest will come from your ability to fix more than just one allergy.

But don't you see what's about to unfold?
When customers come to your allergy clinic, they will probably have two, three, even five allergies. And once you've detected the allergies, you can advise those customers to come back and fix the rest of the allergies.

And similarly in your website strategy workshop, you're more than likely to deal with attraction, conversion and customer retention. Or have other workshops that deal with these topics.

The customer needs to be alerted to a single problem at a time. And the customer has to be taken through one 'room at a time.'

Yes, you have many 'rooms' in your home. And each room represents a product/ service. But when someone enters your home, do you rush them through all the rooms? Or do you take them through a front door?

The front door could be any of your products or services. First get them through the front door. Then move the customers systematically through the rest of your products and services.

One room at a time. Trying to take someone through every room in your house is quite a silly strategy. Isolate the room that's most interesting to the customer, before showing them the rest of the rooms.

Isolation is the equivalent of dog poo on a crowded street.
The equivalent of a block of wood headed towards your head. The equivalent of a police car on a busy highway.

Pain and problems are a natural magnet for the brain. We can see how they instantly get our attention in our day to day lives. We should be using the power of problems in all our communication, marketing and advertising. Yet what do we do instead? We don't use the problem. We revert to the solution.

Why on earth do we do that? Why revert to the solution when it's clear that the problem does indeed capture the imagination of the brain? And what's the role of the solution?

Let's find out, shall we?

Summary: The Problem

- The Problem gets our instant attention. This is because our brain is always on the lookout for the problem. While solutions may or may not engage the brain, a problem always gets the brain's attention.

- The level of the attention of the brain depends on the problem at hand. The brain goes through distinct steps. It recognises change; recognises that change is indeed a problem worth looking at; works out the severity of the problem; finally works out the action it needs to take.

- Customers have dozens of problems running rampant in their brains. The way a business can get a customer's attention is by isolating the problem.

- Isolating the problem means you literally flag a customer down by specifying that customer's problem. For example: 'are you allergic to cats?' would be the way to flag down a customer who suspects he's allergic to cats.

- Isolating the problem may seem like a counter-intuitive thing to do. Why wouldn't you flag down a customer by talking about 'allergies', instead of the more specific 'allergic to cats'? The reason is simple. The customer is more likely to respond to specifics. And once the customer has responded, you can then show the customer the rest of your products/services.

- This method of isolating the problem, and then introducing the customer to other problems that need solving, can be best described by an analogy of a home. You have many rooms in your home, but you get your customer through the door, and get them to sit in the lounge. Once they're relaxed, you then introduce the customer to the other rooms (other products/services).

- Are we just inventing problems to compel the customer to buy? Are we creating urgency out of nothing at all? Your customer isn't a fool. He/She knows what he/she wants. When you present the problem in the right manner, that want is elevated, and is given a sense of urgency. And that causes the customer not to put off the decision until later, but to take action right away.

The Solution

Why 'solutions' play 'follow the leader'

Bag 2: The Solution

Problems attract attention. Of that we seem to be pretty sure by now.

So should we simply drop 'the solution' like a hot potato? And why would *the solution* be important? And just what is 'the solution' in the first place?

First let's get the definition out of the way.
The solution is simply the answer to the problem. The customer has 'a problem'. You bring up 'the solution'. The customer has an issue that needs fixing. You're the fix-it person. The solution is simply the answer to a need or want that the customer has.

But notice something. We seem to depend a lot on solutions when describing our products or services. When someone asks you what you do, you always answer in the form of a solution.

So if you were in the lawn-mowing business and someone asked you what you do for a living, you'd say something like: 'I mow lawns'. Or if you are selling a product such as writing paper, you'd say: 'I help people find exquisite writing paper'.

These statements are 'solution statements'. So why is it that we use so many 'solution statements', when our brains instinctively react to 'problem statements'? We use solution statements for one specific reason.

See how the solution is kinda weak? Because as a customer, you need to know what's wrong with 'the chairs' in the first place. Solutions do a great job, but they need to follow the problem to create impact.

We've been trained to state the benefits and features.
Most of us have either read somewhere, or been told, to state the benefits and features of a product/service.

And benefits and features are synonymous with 'solution statements'. They simply tell us what to expect in a product or service, and how to apply those features in our everyday life. And since benefits and features have worked so well for us in the past, we continue to use benefits and features. So what are we to do, now that we know the power of 'the problem'?

Are we to simply drop the solution?
Not at all. We simply follow the sequence of the bags.

First the problem.
Then the solution.
And I suspect you know why I'm insisting on this sequence, but I'll explain anyway. Our brains are always on the lookout for a possible problem. And so they're attracted to the problem first. But when a brain runs into a problem, it also gets pretty anxious. And it's only when it sees the obvious—and possibly the most appropriate solution—that it starts to relax.

You tend not to notice a solution, if you don't have a problem in the first place. That puppy doesn't scare you at all. But if it were a big, snarly bulldog headed your way, you'd be racing towards a 'solution' instantly.

So if you were walking in the park, and this big snarling dog was headed your way, your brain would instantly be activated. And in a matter of seconds your brain would be scrambling to find a solution. The scramble would cause you to be agitated, increasing your heart rate instantly. If you did manage to duck into an enclosed area and shut the gate behind you, you'd feel immediate relief.

This is the role of the solution: to bring relief.
But let's jump the sequence a bit. Let's say there was no dog. Let's assume you were walking through the park on a day when nothing went wrong. Would you pay attention to the enclosed area in the park? Would you bother going inside? Or would you continue your leisurely walk?

You probably wouldn't have noticed the enclosed area even though you've passed it several times before. And yet, as this four-legged menace heads towards you, you're now paying attention to something you've never really paid attention to before: the enclosed area with the nice, secure gate.

The nice, secure gate is what your customer is looking for as well. When the customer is faced with a problem, he or she's looking for a solution. But the customer's brain is not just looking for the solution, it's also looking for whether you as a supplier of products/ services understands its owner's problem. So let's take another example to see how the problem and the solution act in tandem with each other.

Let's say it's a hot, humid day.
And you're helping two adorable kids sell cold, lip-smacking lemonade.

Let's also assume that your lemonade stand is clean, tidy and your signs are well displayed. And then, just for good measure, you've got these sweet kids with the cutest 'buy-my-lemonade' looks on their faces.

Would this mean that most of the people passing by would no longer stop and drink your reasonably-priced lemonade? If you think that most passersby would stop and drink the lemonade, you'd be right.

Given the right conditions and the right packaging and display, many would stop for the lemonade because it provides a relief (solution) to the hot and humid day. But we fail to take one little factor into consideration.

That in any market, there isn't just one product or service to contend with.
In every market, you have ten, twenty, or even five hundred lemonade stands on the same sidewalk. And if your sign is simply a

solution, like all the other signs, then the customer's brain may simply not react to your sign. But a sign with a problem gets attention.

In just about any market, there are going to be competitors. And you can bet your socks that most of your competitors won't understand the concept of the problem and solution. They'll simply sell the solution: 'Lemonade'. But a sign that says: 'Germ-conscious?: Filtered lemonade' stands out immediately because it's highlighting a problem before the solution.

The solution keeps that attention.
So no, the solution can't be dropped like a hot potato. The solution does indeed have a place. And its rightful place is right after you've brought up the problem. Once the problem has been activated in the customer's brain, it's imperative to bring up the solution.

But there's a difference between the solution and the process.

So what's the difference?
The process is the method you use to solve a problem. The solution, on the other hand, is simply the answer to the problem.

Let's take an example.
Let's go back to the allergy centre example.
When someone asks you what you do, you may say: "If you're allergic to pollen, I help you get rid of your allergy forever". Now that's a problem and solution (and target profile) rolled in one statement. And instantly it gets the attention of the prospective customers.

But what if you were to describe a process instead of a solution?
Here's what a process would sound like: *Our solution is to use the glramoxcotyhinx testing device, to determine the speed of your body*

cells and to enable your natural defense mechanism to go 230 cycles quicker than before, and yada, yada, yada.

Ugh!

That's not a solution. That's a process. We're not interested in your process, We have 'a problem': We 'achoo' when we come into contact with pollen (and vice versa). Your *solution* should be: *You help me get rid of the allergy.* We do not care how you do what you do, and what crazy devices you use. At this point, the only solution we're interested in is to stop me from #@$%^$%# sneezing all day long!

Your process may be very, very interesting. But the customer is or interested in the solution for now. So yeah, stow that process away for now.

In effect, your 'solution statement' should be the mirror-image of the problem statement. So if the problem is getting *stuck indoors,* the solution is *going outdoors.* If the problem is a *backache,* the solution is the *lack of the backache.* If the problem is *frenzied dog attacks,* your solution is *protection from frenzied dog attacks.* It's the sequence of the problem followed by the solution that makes the message so very effective.

But how do we know that problems and solutions need to follow in sequence?
We see proof of this problem/solution activity every night on television.

It's called the News. So if you were to watch the 6pm news tonight, what do you think would be the first item on the news? Yup, it would be the biggest problem of the day.

And what would be the second item on the news?
Naturally, it's the second biggest problem of the day. And so the news would progress steadily 'til you reach the *puppy dog* stories. So when do you get to hear about the warm, fuzzy news stories?

Yes, right at the end of the news. And why do you think that is so? You guessed right. If all you did was have puppy dog stories at 6pm, you'd never watch the news.

What's more, this phenomenon is not restricted to 6pm.
Read your newspaper, or switch to any online news report and notice what's making the headlines today. Go to the supermarket and glance at what the gossip magazines have plastered across the front page. You'll find that someone's divorcing someone, or someone's been arrested, or someone's gone and done something really, really naughty.

In fact, you'll soon find that almost every media outlet from the radio, to television, to magazines uses the power of 'the problem' to get your attention. And the reason why they use the power of 'the problem', is because the brain is focused on 'the problem' . The brain learns to recognise a problem, long before it sees a solution.

And yet, the vast majority of businesses insist on using a solution to get their message across. All you have to do is simply open your newspaper on any day of the week, and these are the kind of ads you'd see:

Enjoy amazing harbour views - Restaurant
Tell everyone about your event - Public Relations
Sleep soundly - Bed Company
Create your own web page - Web Training
Enjoy a career in diving - Dive School

If you don't isolate the problem, 'all roads' look the same to the customer. And they fail to pay attention to your product or service offering.

What was your reaction when you saw these ads?
Did they get you extremely excited? Did they compel you to find out more? If you're like most people, most–if not all– of these ads would have been close to invisible. Whoosh, your eyes would have gone past them in a blur.

So what does get your attention in the newspaper?
Editorial surely would. All that doom and gloom about the cat burglar who was pillaging your neighbourhood would get your attention. Did you notice how your eye went to the *increase in taxes*? Or the little child that has gone missing? And yes, if there was an ad that was smart enough to create a problem, you'd be noticing that product or service for sure.

So yes, problems start the sequence.
They get your attention. But if you overdid the problems, your customers would be so intimidated that they'd actually avoid dealing with you. Which is why the solution has to come to the rescue as quickly as possible.

The problem isn't more important than the solution. It's just that the problem comes first in the sequence, and then the solution follows shortly after.

And let's briefly go back to our examples from the first chapter:
Example 1: Website strategy workshop
Example 2: An allergy clinic

Website strategy workshop

Problem: *Are you sick and tired of internet systems that force you to become a 'monster'? (Most internet-training systems 'convince' you to do things that you think are 'yucky'. They make you believe that the only way to get sales, is to use methods that border on 'sleazy behaviour'. So is there a way to be ethical and still bring in growing amounts of revenue?)*

Solution: *Here's how to create a website strategy that's ethical, yet extremely profitable.*

An allergy clinic

Problem: *Do you find yourself sneezing after one or two glasses of wine? Do you find that you literally launch into a sneezing fit and have to take an anti-allergy pill every single time?*

Solution: *Here's how you can get rid of the allergic reaction in less than 24 hours (and without any pills or medication whatsoever).*

As you can see, we've isolated the problem from the last chapter. And simply presented the solution to that very problem, without trying to be too creative or clever.

Not being too creative or clever is important, because the customer is not looking for a clever answer. They have a problem. You've identified the problem. They want a solution. Give them the solution.

The solution is the flip side of the problem.
If the customer's computer is slow, you're speeding it up. If the customer's mattress is too spongy, you're providing a well-supported mattress. If the customer's paying too much for their airfares, you're providing a low-price alternative.

If you try to be clever with the solution, you'll confuse the customer. The solution is just the flip side of the problem.

There's nothing clever about the solution. There shouldn't be. All the solution should do is flip the problem around.

Which takes us to Bag No.3.
At this very moment we realise that two bags have come off that conveyor belt. And there's the third bag slowly edging its way towards us. The bag called the 'target profile'.

Avoid the temptation to bring up the 'solution' first. First problems, then solutions.

If you don't spend time working out your target profile, you may as well waffle your way through your sales and marketing, forever. The difference between a *great* sales and marketing message, and a good one, is an understanding of target profile.

So pay very, very close attention as we pick Bag No.3 from the conveyor belt.

Summary: The Solution

- Solutions are just as important as problems. But they have to follow the sequence. They should only show up once the problem has been introduced. Don't jump the gun and put your solution before the problem. Doing so will greatly reduce the impact of the communication.

- Solutions are pain-relievers. They bring down the 'pressure cooker situation' created by the problem. They assure the customer that there is a light at the end of the tunnel.

- Audit your communication rigorously for solutions popping up first. Your natural tendency will be to put a solution first. Resist that temptation and keep it second.

- The solution is different from the process. The client is not interested in how you do things—well, not at the start anyway. The role of the solution is to nullify the problem, not to explain the long-winded process you use.

- The solution is the flip side of the problem. There's no need to be clever about the solution. If customers have rain falling on their heads, you're providing a raincoat. A 'rain-repellent plastic covering' would be a clever description. And being too clever simply confuses your customer and drives him away.

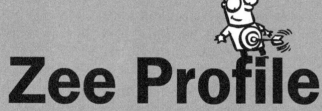

Zee Profile

Can't we just market to everyone? Why must we choose?

Bag 3: The Target Profile

Let's say you've been given an assignment.
You've been told a relative is turning fifty this year.
And you're not sure, but you guess he might like to have a *TIME*
magazine cover. A cover that gives him a sense of what was
happening in the exact week he was born.

So what are you going to do?
Are you simply going to go back fifty years, and pick any cover? Of
course not! Why would you do that? You'd first do some digging,
wouldn't you? You'd first find out which month that relative was
born. Then you'd find out which day, so you could accurately locate
the week. And only once you had those details would you let your
credit card take the hit.

But suppose you got the details only marginally wrong.
What if the person was born on the 1st of November, and you got a
cover that just missed that date—and happened to be a cover of the
week before the 1st of November. Would that do? I mean it's close
enough, eh? What's the big deal? But even as
you're saying 'big deal', you know that the cover
you managed to purchase—close as it to the
date—is miles away. The only cover that will
make the gift perfect, is a cover that includes
the exact week in which the 'birthday-boy' was
born.

But notice something else. Notice that our
'birthday-boy' wasn't the only person born in
that particular week. Or that particular day.
On that day/week, there would have been
thousands, or tens of thousands of crying ba-
bies who shared the same date/week of birth.
For all of whom the *TIME* magazine cover
would be spot-on.

If you wanted to play
Santa and get a gift
just right, you'd be in
big trouble if you didn't
know exactly what the
person wanted. Playing
Santa requires you
to understand 'target
profile', in order to do a
great job of gifting.

And then again, it might not be spot-on after all.

Because we're not talking about an audience.
We're talking about one person.
One person who would actually appreciate getting a *TIME* cover.

The concept of 'target audience' is misleading, because while audiences may appear to be similar, their individual needs may vary wildly.

I might.
You might.

But the 'birthday-boy' may actually be looking forward to a *PLAYBOY* cover instead of a *TIME* cover. Or no cover at all. And despite your best intentions, you've only been guessing about the relevance of the gift. While you've got the whole issue of *'target audience'* quite right, you've got the profile horribly wrong. What you need to have isn't quite an audience, but a 'target profile' instead. So the question must arise: what is this strange term that goes by the name of 'target profile'?

Target profile is simply the factor of choosing one person.
Not an entire audience.
But one solitary person.
And then crafting your message to that one person.

Of course, you don't believe me.
Trying to send a message to just one person seems like marketing suicide.

But suspend your disbelief for a while, and read on. Because we need to understand how to construct a 'target profile'. And to make sure we construct a great profile, we need to start with the difference between 'target profile' and 'target audience'.

And a good place to start is the concept of 'target audience'. What indeed is a 'target audience'?

We can answer this question quite simply if we take a sample of three women sitting in a café. Let's assume they're all in their 30's. They all live in the same neighbourhood. They all went to the same schools, even the same university and graduated in the same year. All of them have the average of 2.2 kids. They all like wearing jeans. They all love buying shoes. And if you look at the data on paper, they seem alike.

And marketers call this 'factor of similarity' a 'target audience'. And they label it with the term 'demographics'. A demographic is essentially a segregation of a group of people on the basis of what makes them similar. So if they've got certain similarities then you put them aside and you say, "Hey, these are women, same neighbourhood, same university, kids, jeans, shoes, etc."

On paper they all look alike.

Well, let's suppose you wanted to sell jeans to these women. Now you know that they like jeans, because hey, there they were in the cafe, and they were all wearing jeans. On paper a sale of this nature would seem simple. But there's a bit of a problem that crops up.

And the problem is very simple. The first woman weighs 107 pounds (which is 49 kilos). The second woman weighs 132 pounds (which is 60 kilos). The third woman weighs 200 pounds (which is 91 kilos). And that's just their weight. Not their height or shape.

Yes, you're selling a generic product like jeans. And you're selling it to a demographic. Logically, you should be able to sell it to all of these three women, without a problem.

But to your frustration you find that the women aren't really buying jeans. They're buying into a solution. And to work out the solution, we first have to define the problem. One woman may be considering the comfort of the jeans as the top priority. Another is considering colour. The third may be considering the cut.

Each one will be buying her jeans on a completely different parameter. And that parameter is paramount to them. In fact, that parameter will come before all other parameters.

All very fine when you're considering three women in a cafe. But hey, does this profiling actually work? Does it actually make money? Does it actually get customers?

For this we have to go back to Brighton, England.
In the year 1976, Anita Roddick started a tiny little store in Brighton, England. It was a cheeky little store called 'The Body Shop'. Cheeky because as Anita herself said, "It was hard (to start up). It was breathtakingly funny. I was stuck between two funeral parlours who objected to the name The Body Shop because coffins would pass by a couple of times a day."

The Body Shop didn't target all women. It targeted women who were against cosmetics being tested on animals. The targeting was based on a specific profile.

Despite the rather ordinary name, it's not the products that got the attention of its customers—and subsequently the attention of the world's press. Because you see, Anita's products were simply beauty products for women.

And beauty products are a dime a dozen today, as they were back in 1976.
Yet, Anita wasn't talking to all women. She wasn't even speaking to women who used beauty products. But instead she spoke to a specific problem. At the time—and even possibly today—the ingredients of beauty products were tested on animals. And Anita was tackling this specific issue: the problem of ethical consumerism.

We know little about the funeral parlours. But we do know that Anita Roddick went on to create a business that millions of women were attracted to. And in the year 2006, when Anita finally decided to sell the business to L'Oréal, she did so for a cool fee of £652 million!

Think about it. A tiny business. A business not a heck of a lot different from those funeral parlours that were simply appealing to a demographic. Yet Anita changed it all by appealing to a profile. And it's this profiling (among other things) that catapulted The Body Shop into the brand that it is today.

What works for cosmetics works just as well for products and services.
From products such as tractors, to ball bearings, to services such as marketing, consulting or workshops.

There's not one product/service on this planet that can't be sharpened with precise profiling. And precise profiling works on the basis of one person.

Like my wife, Renuka. When Renuka goes out to buy shoes, she runs into a massive problem. Like every other woman, she likes her shoes. But she's got tiny feet, and hence she spends loads of time simply going from shoe-shop to shoe-shop in search of her size.

Is there a market for Size 5 shoes? You wouldn't think so, would you? Yet even a casual search on the internet brings up several sites based on a specific 'target profile'.

Now just like every other woman, she's concerned about colour, fit, shape, comfort, etc. But what good is that laundry list when she can't even get her size? So what is Renuka's dream? To find a store that's called 'The Renuka Shoe Store'. And in that store, they stock just Size 5 shoes. From the top to bottom, they have Size 5, in every colour, every type, every material, every level of comfort and for every occasion.

Imagine a store like that. Do you think that Renuka would even bother going to another shoe store?

But surely you think, that's ridiculous.
Building a business around one person is insane. Surely you can't hope to earn a living creating such a tiny niche. But is it a tiny niche? Because how many 'Renukas' exist in the city of Auckland? How many 'Renukas' exist in New Zealand? And how many of them exist on this side of the planet, let alone the entire world?

Could you open a vegetarian-only pizza parlour? Do you think vegetarians would pay a little more just to make sure that there's no chance of any meat in sight at the pizzeria? There are a dozen or more niches for everything, y'know! And the good news is: all the niches aren't taken yet.

They must exist, and it must be reasonably profitable, because even a casual search at Google throws up sites all over the world. In five seconds, I was able to find *www.feetpetite.co.nz, www.daintyfeet.com, www.cinderellaofboston.com, www.small-shoes.co.uk*, and *www.zappos.com*. And believe me, I wasn't even really trying to research the subject thoroughly. I just clicked on the first link that Google threw up.

It does seem that there exists a market—and a profitable market too—for a business built on the profile of one person. We see this market when we look at The Body Shop—which incidentally started out as just one store, and not a global corporation. We see this as we look at shoe stores which cater to women who have the problem of finding shoes for tiny feet.

And yet we have to understand that there are more shoe stores that cater to general audiences, and still do well. They too make profits. They too have nice balance sheets. But there's a slight difference when you build a business on the basis of a specific profile.

And that difference is one of specifics.
That when you build a business with one person in mind, you attract hundreds, thousands, even millions of customers. In fact, you don't have to go far to see how this concept of profiling was used, and continues to be used.

On September 7, 1998, an unknown company called Google was privately registered while the founders Larry Page and Sergey Brin were still at Stanford University. Google was unknown at the time as a search engine. And if you looked around, there were tons of search engines. They went by the names of HotBot, Alta Vista, Yahoo!, Magellan, Lycos, Infoseek and Excite (amongst others).

So how did Google stand out from this gaggle of search engines? It stood out with its clear interface. When you went to Google.com, you only had one box to fill; one thing to see. The profile was clearly a person who was sick and tired of having to deal with clutter. Google was designed for a person who despised the clutter.

And you know the rest of the story, don't you?
Armed with that early boost, Google.com[1] has gone on to become one of the biggest brand names on the planet. And yes, they had good search algorithms. And yes, they did this and did that, but at the very core they appealed to a profile. Which then ballooned into an audience. Which now pretty much has ballooned into half the planet.

Target profiling works.

All you need to know is how to use it to your advantage. And that's what we're about to find out.

---

[1] In case you're wondering, this book has no connection with The Body Shop or Google. The only connection is the analysis of the thought process that would have gone into creating a 'target profile'.

Creating a Profile

Let's start at the top: how do you create a profile?
Step 1: Start with a demographic
Step 2: Choose a real person from that demographic
Step 3: Speak to that person and find out their list of problems (with regard to a product/service)
Step 4: Choose one problem then expand it
Step 5: Use a real person to get feedback.

So let me explain how all of this works.
Imagine you're looking for a date on a website such as Match.com. What you do is start with a demographic. You're either a guy looking for a girl. Or a girl looking for a guy. Or a girl looking for a girl, or a guy looking for a guy. Those are essentially the parameters. Or the demographics.

Step 1: Choose a demographic.
The first thing you have to start off with is a demographic. A demographic is what will give you an idea of whether you're speaking to a specific age group, specific profession, etc. And we saw a demographic of a group of women earlier. They were people who liked their coffee, went to the same university, 2.2 kids, wearing jeans, shoes, etc. That's a demographic. And so we get this demographic when we're looking for this 'ideal mate' on Match.com.

But there's a problem instantly. Because if you were to search for demographics, you'd instantly get twenty dozen people who fit your 'demographic' description. And even if they all look like your ideal man/woman, you've got a big problem if you try and contact all of them.

So you move to Step 2: Choose a real person.
You've moved from the 'drop down boxes' where you chose age/city/country in order to find someone whom you were looking

for. Now you're scanning for something. On Match.com you'll be scanning for faces to begin with. And soon you'll find that real person. Or the profile of that real person. And you'll start to read more about that real person. And want to contact that real person. But do you see what's happening? You've stepped out of the 'perfect person' zone and stepped into the 'real person' zone.

Aha, Step 3: See the criteria/needs/problems of that real person.
Of course they don't call it problems on Match.com. They call it criteria, or 'About Me'. Then this person tells us what he/she really wants. And doesn't want.

And then it's Step 4: Expanding the criterion.
Get the person to choose one criterion that he's/she's really interested in.

And I can tell you right away, that there are twenty-dozen criteria. But if he's/she's really smart, or really keen, he's/she's bound to tell you that one thing that he/she is really interested in. That's what you need to pay attention to, because as I said, 'he/she will tell you'. You need to talk to your profile to get the one problem out. You can't afford to sit at your desk imagining the problems the 'target profile' could/should have. You have to talk.

You then stop fiddling around with all the criteria and focus on that one criterion. That one thing is bigger, more important than everything else. And you hone in, and talk to him/her about that one thing over and over, until you know everything there is to know about that one criterion.

Then you feed it back to the person in Step 5.
Ask them if that one criterion is what he/she wants. Brainstorm with your 'target profile' to flesh out the one problem they've identified. And watch as his/her eyes twinkle. If you're saying the right thing you'll get delight in the voice.

You'll get excitement.

If you're sitting in front of that person, you'll see the gentle nod of the head. But if you're saying the wrong thing, that person will sound confused. Or be scowling just a tiny bit. This playing back of the biggest issue to the person is critical to find out if you've indeed heard what he's/she's 'actually' been saying—and that you're not hearing what you want to hear.

When you've gone through all the five steps, you've now got a very decent idea of how to create a profile. When we profile real clients, we have to follow the very same system. And just for good measure, let's take an example of a real person, and go through those five steps once more. This time we'll use a real client (notice how many times I'm saying the word 'real'.)

Going through the five steps with a real client.
Let's start off at the top. We choose the demographic. And that demographic is women looking to buy shoes.

Now from that demographic, let's choose a real person. We choose a real person like Renuka. And we say, "OK fine. There are 50 women or 100 women or 2,000 women in this suburb, and we're going to choose one person in order to get to a profile".

And then we either call Renuka or we sit down with her over her favourite 'iced-coffee', and we talk to her about shoes. And what are her criteria for buying shoes. List all the criteria. And the problems she has with getting shoes. As you talk to her, you'll get the usual list: size, comfort, colour, etc. And now it's time to get Renuka to tell you which one of those problems is the biggest—and most frustrating of them all.

And it's at this point that things get really interesting.
Because this is the part where we get the terminology, the emotion, the logic, the 'everything' from the customer. In her own words. And believe me, you don't want to stop her talking. Let her do the talking. You do the recording. Do the questioning. And do the writing.

Let her talk, because she's going to tell you things you could never make up sitting at your desk. And if you give her enough time, she's going to tell you the real reason why she wants those shoes.

You take that information and you create your sales page.
You take that information and you write your article. You take that information and create your presentation. Because that person has gone from a vague 'target audience', to a real person with a real list of problems.

And then you move to the feedback stage.
You read back what you've heard. And watch the expression and body language. Listen to the tone of voice. You're asking for feedback. You want to pay close attention to make sure that you've actually heard what you've heard.

And you've got a profile. A profile that's individual to Renuka. A profile like no other.

Which brings us back to our two examples:
Example 1: Website strategy workshop
Example 2: An allergy clinic

Website strategy workshop

Target Profile: Howard R.

Howard is a real person. He sells products and services on the internet but wasn't sure how to go forward. The words are his. He told me, "I didn't feel like a monster, but in order to 'play the game' at the highest level I'd have to become one, or at least act like one. I never got to the point where I was doing anything that disgusted me. I just couldn't see a path to growth that didn't involve 'guru bullshit'".

Problem: *Are you sick and tired of internet systems that force you to become a 'monster'? (Most internet-training systems 'convince' you to do* *things that you think are yucky. They make you believe, the only way to get sales, is to use methods that border on 'sleazy behaviour'. So is there a way to be ethical and still bring in growing amounts of revenue?*

Solution: *Here's how to create a website strategy that's ethical, yet extremely profitable.*

An allergy clinic

Target Profile: Tricia M.

Tricia M. is a pseudonym for a real person. Tricia found that at about 8pm, she'd start sneezing. At first she suspected it was a reaction to dust, or pets. But over time she realised she was sneezing after a couple of glasses of wine. She'd start to sneeze. Then her eyes would get itchy. Then she'd have to dig in her handbag for anti-allergy pills. She hated the fact that she loved drinking wine, but had to abstain simply because of the fear of an endless number of 'achoos'!

Problem: *Do you find yourself sneezing after one or two glasses of wine? Do you find that you literally launch into a sneezing fit and have to take an anti-allergy pill every single time?*

Solution: *Here's how you can get rid of the allergic reaction in less than 24 hours (and without any pills or medication whatsoever).*

Yes, I know you noticed that the 'target profile' came before the problem and solution.

First you need to know whom you're speaking to. That conversation leads to a clear profile where you get a specific problem. And a specific solution. And yippee-yahooey, we're well on our way.

Or are we? You may feel that you're doing fine with the concept of 'target audience'. Is target profiling right for you? Let's find out.

A martini designed for just one playboy on the planet. What kind of marketer would create a James Bond kind of martini? And who would drink it? You know the answer. Every person who aspires to be James Bond, would want a martini just like Bond drinks. And of course, the suit to match.

The Profiling Journey

Okay, so profiling a client is starting to make a lot of sense.

If you were starting up a new business, that is.

If you didn't have so many different clients, that is. If you weren't already selling products/services, that is.

There are several reasons why you may love target profiling—and the clarity it brings—but still be unsure of how to implement it for your business. So let's look at the situations where we run into target profiling, and see how we can implement it for your business.

There are several reasons why you may think that target profiling doesn't seem to work.
These situations are:
1) Won't target profiling really start to exclude people?
2) What if I already have a sales message that seems to work for me?
3) What if I already have several audiences that seem to buy my product/service?
4) What if I have multiple products/services?
5) What if my products/services solve multiple problems?

Let's take a simple analogy of a bullseye to answer all of these questions. And then take a case study where a real business owner is trying to get a message across to his client in the most effective manner possible.

Why aim for the bullseye, when you can hit any spot on the dart board?

Question 1: Won't target profiling really start to exclude people?
If you were throwing darts on a dart board, what are you aiming for?
The bullseye, right? Well, why would you want to do that? There's
the entire board. You could throw the dart just about anywhere.
Yet, you exclude the rest of the board, aiming only for the bullseye.
You do this because you know the bullseye gets you the maximum
number of points. And so it is with profiling. You could try to
include everyone (include any part of the dartboard, that is), and
yet focusing on your bullseye is what gives you maximum impact.

If you want to get maximum impact you're going to have to exclude
people. Strangely, the more niche you make your product/service
seem, the more you'll find people attracted to it. Just like on a
board, where the tiniest part of the board seems to attract the
largest number of dart-throwers.

Question 2: What if I already have a message that's working for me?
You probably do. And on the dartboard, you can not hit the bullseye
and still get points. Does that answer your question? The key is to
get the maximum impact. If you're happy with reduced impact, you
can continue to sell as you've always sold. It's not that your product/
service won't sell. It's just a factor of impact.

**Question 3: What if I already have several audiences that seem to
buy my product/service?**
Every product/service has several audiences. Think about the
board. Do only Guinness-swilling guys throw darts on the board?
No, Heineken-swilling guys do too. And so do Steinlager-swilling
guys. And Kingfisher-swilling guys. And non-beer-swilling guys.

And not just guys. But girls. And women. And kids. And yes, there
are going to be several audiences. We call them target audiences.

But what problem does the dartboard serve? It depends on the 'target
profile', doesn't it? Because the problem it solves for kids isn't the
problem it solves over a margarita party, is it? So that still leaves us with
the problem of several audiences. And we'll answer that in Answer 5.

Question 4: What if I already have multiple products/services?
Let's drag that bullseye back into the picture and you're going to have several colours to choose from. Several parts of the board. Well, the board is separate from the wall, you see.

The wall represents pretty much everything that's possible in your field.

The board represents your company and profile. And you can have many products and services, as you've seen in the case studies. You just have to pick a profile for each of those products and services in order to attract the right audience.

Every business has many products and services. And each product or service will have many audiences. In today's world, it's easy to tackle all those audiences—one at a time.

But what if you have thousands of products/services for sale? Would you pick a profile for every darned product/service? Hey, yeah. You don't have to do it now, but each product/service has a maximum impact point. And customers have limited bandwidth. They will pay attention to your product/service, only if you get, and keep, their attention. If you waffle, you'll miss the bullseye.

A good start would be to work with your best-sellers, in order to make them even better-selling. And then work your way down to products/services that aren't so hot.

Question 5: But what if my products/services solve multiple problems?
Your product or service will solve multiple problems. See that dart board. When you get really good at communicating your product/service, you get really good at throwing multiple darts on the bullseye. So heck yeah, you will get all your darts on a bullseye. And today's technology allows you to send out several messages to different audiences.

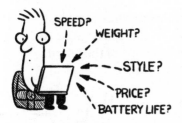

Every product will solve multiple problems. Yet if you base your marketing on individual profiles, each message will be far more powerful than if you simply try to get every single problem across in the same message.

So if you have five bullseye messages, and want to attract different people through your website, you can create five landing pages. If you've got five bullseye messages and want to create five different brochures, you can do so with little effort thanks to digital printing.

You can create five different videos, audio files, booklets, screensavers, etc. The world is digital. You can, if you choose to, put your five bullseye messages into several separate media and packaging options with just a little work on your part.

Case Study

Which brings us to a real case-study (and gets us off that darned dartboard!)
Greg from the holistic healing centre solves several problems.
1) Migraines
2) Chronic Lyme Disease
3) Insomnia
4) Weight-Loss
5) Fibromyalgia.

Let's ask the questions again:
1) Won't target profiling really start to exclude people?
2) What if I already have a sales message that seems to work for me?
3) What if I already have several audiences that seem to buy my product/service?
4) What if I have multiple products/services?
5) What if my products/services solve multiple problems?

If he focuses on just fibromyalgia, will he start to exclude people?
You bet he will. Is it a good idea? Hey, that's a rhetorical question. He could be the *mecca* of healing for fibromyalgia sufferers. But he already has customers and already has a sales message, and already has several audiences. Sure he does.

But what if he could focus on the bullseye of fibromyalgia? Because this is what fibromyalgia sufferers go through. And to quote Greg: *Fibromyalgia clients are not getting better. They live a nightmarish existence:*
- feeling like a doped-up zombie on medications
- exhausted by lack of sleep
- wracked by daily chronic pain that gets worse with the wrong food, wet weather, strong emotions
- hopelessly depressed about their future of more pain, fatigue
- other complications like arthritis, osteoporosis, addictions.

So if we were to isolate just the factor of pain from the list above, we'd still get a lot to choose from.

- wracked by daily chronic pain that gets worse with the wrong food
- wracked by daily chronic pain that gets worse with the wet weather
- wracked by daily chronic pain that gets worse with strong emotions
- wracked by daily chronic pain that causes extreme fatigue.

So yes, Greg's service solves many problems and appeals to many audiences. Yet it's only by profiling that we learn to focus on that bullseye. And yes, with today's digital technology, it's easy for Greg to have five different signs in the same vicinity of his healing centre.

Five signs with five specific messages. And each message appeals to a different profile. The profile may all have the same problem: namely fibromyalgia, and yet, it's the specificity of the problem that will cause them to choose one problem over the other.

By aiming for the bullseye, we're eliminating 90% (or more) of the dartboard. Yes, you read right.
The purpose of profiling is indeed meant to 'exclude' customers who don't fit the profile. And does it work? You bet it does!

Remember one other thing. It's not always the profile that's looking out for your product/service. Our partners, friends, relatives are all looking for a product/service that will solve their own issues. But they're also looking out for a product/service that may help you.

While you as the exact profile may know and recognise all the symptoms, it's possible that your partners/friends/relatives aren't that clear about your multiple symptoms. And even in their minds, one thing will be higher priority than the other. E.g. *Wet weather* vs. *food*. Or *wet weather* vs. *strong emotions*.

And while they may recognise the *wet weather* message, they may completely ignore the food message. Your ability to communicate single-mindedly is what makes the difference. If you choose to have one sign and depend on that one sign, then go for it.

If you choose to have twenty thousand signs with twenty thousand symptoms, then be my guest. Just remember one thing: each sign, each message, should be singularly focused.

That's what makes profiling so interesting.
It's not just a factor of boiling down to one person but then isolating it to one factor E.g. *fibromyalgia*. And then isolating it further to one symptom/problem E.g. *Wet weather that causes fatigue.*

When you are clear whom you're speaking to, the problem becomes clear. And so does the solution. And immediately the muddiness goes out of your communication.

Magical as this understanding of problem, solution and 'target profile' may seem, the magic moves up to a whole new level when you combine the problem, solution and 'target' together.

Because you're about to set off a trigger in the brain of your client. Let's find out how.

Summary: The Target Profile

- There's a difference between 'target audience' and 'target profile'. An audience represents a group of people who seem to have something in common. The 'target profile' is just one person. A real person, with a real name, with a real address, and real phone number. And with real problems.

- And while it's hard enough to restrict yourself to a 'target audience', it seems almost nutty to restrict yourself to a 'target profile'. And yet, restricting yourself to a profile gets you to easily focus on the problems and solutions of that one person with extreme clarity.
To create a profile, we have to take five specific steps:
Step 1: Start with a demographic;
Step 2: Choose a real person from that demographic;
Step 3: Speak to that person and find out the list of problems (with regard to a product/service);
Step 4: Choose one problem then expand it;
Step 5: Use a real person to get feedback.

- Profiling does exclude a lot of people. And conversely it includes people. It excludes those who aren't interested in your product or service. And includes people who are actively searching for your product or service.

- Every product/service appeals to different audiences. And every product/service solves a range of problems. Profiling helps you figure out how you can systematically speak to different audiences using different messages.

- Today's world allows for digital-this and digital-that. It allows you to test your messages more effectively than ever before. And unlike in the past where you had to produce thousands of fliers or signs, you can now create just one message at a time. One flier. One sign. One brochure. One page on a website. And you can easily test which profile draws the biggest audience. That's when you've hit pay dirt!

The Trigger

Ooh, It's time to tickle the brain!

Pop Goes The Trigger!

Some scientist or researcher somewhere worked out that we see about three thousand new messages per day.

Ooh, that's a lot of messages.

But let's suppose we didn't see three thousand new messages.
Let's suppose we saw only seven hundred and fifty. Or maybe two hundred and fifty. Or even fifty.

What would it take for something to cut through those fifty messages? What would it take for the client to ignore the rest of those forty-nine messages and focus on your message?

I'll tell you what.
It's called a trigger. And a trigger is simply the ability of a message to stand out, and get your attention. A trigger instantly gets the attention of the brain. And when faced with the trigger, the brain—your brain or the client's brain—has very little option but to respond in an excruciatingly predictable manner.

When the brain gets a ton of stuff, it only pays attention to what's really important. Or to something that causes intense curiosity.

It's excruciating, because no matter how hard your brain tries, the only set of words it can think of are: 'How do you do that?' or 'What do you mean by that?'. But how do you get the brain to respond so consistently? You get the consistency when you use the combination of 'the problem, solution and target' in one phrase or sentence. Let's look at three examples to see how a trigger is set off.

Example: Yoga centre (training)
Target: New mums
Problem: Loss of pre-baby figure
Solution: Get back pre-baby figure
Trigger: *We help new mums quickly get back their pre-baby figure.*

Example: Recruitment agency (service)
Target: Small businesses that want part-time staff
Problem: Big fees
Solution: Get part-time staff without paying big fees.
Trigger: *We help small businesses get part-time staff without paying big fees.*

Example: Face cream (product)
Target: 50 year-olds/ 50+/soon to be 50/ or even 40+
Problem: Looking like a 50 year-old
Solution: Looking like a 30 year-old
Trigger: *How to look 30 when you're 50*

So yeah, when you put the problem, solution and target together, you get a trigger every single time. Or do you? Actually, you don't. Just stringing the trio of problem, solution and target won't always create a trigger. And there's a reason why.

So let's take an example, and let's deliberately water-down one of the three elements that make the trigger.

Target: Women who want to improve their fitness
Problem: Women who are feeling unfit
Solution: A system to get women fitter again
Trigger: *We help women improve their fitness.*

By not concentrating on a niche, we're watering down the trigger. And it's easy to see that despite following the rules of 'trigger-construction', we find that the curiosity factor is missing. We're no longer compelled to say: *'How do you do that?'* or *'What do you mean by that?'* . The trigger is no longer compelling.

And when you water down the trigger, you get the 'kiss of death'.
So what's the 'kiss of death?'. When you run the trigger past a potential client he/she says something like:
1) *That's nice*
2) *Hmmm*
3) *That's interesting.*

What the client has told you—very diplomatically of course—is that you've not piqued their curiosity at all. It may well be that the client is interested in what you have to offer, but in trying to appeal to a broad target profile you've failed to set off the trigger despite getting the 'trigger-construction' technically right.

If you fail to set off the trigger in the customer's mind, they'll make polite conversation with you, and then quickly slink away.

When correctly deployed, the trigger bypasses the 'kiss of death', and gives you permission to continue with your sales message. Because when a client asks you: "What do you mean by that?" they're actually saying, "Tell me more".

And it's time to tell them more, by reverting back to the 'problem' all over again.

The 'problem' all over again? Why are we going backwards?

Remember that police car?
The one that caused you to slow down when you saw the red and blue flashing lights? Well, imagine a situation where you indeed pass the police car, and then come across a giant sign that says: 'No cop car for the next 100km. Guaranteed'.

No cop car for the next 100 km! Hey, would you slow down or speed up? It's the 'cop-car' that makes sure you stay alert. In your message, the 'cop-car' is the 'problem' that pops up ever so often.

What are you going to do?

You know it as well as I do. You're going to speed up, aren't you? And why did you speed up? Because the problem has gone away. You no longer feel the threat of getting a speeding ticket. And that's exactly how a customer feels if you don't implement the roller coaster effect.

So what's the roller coaster effect?

Even if you haven't actually been on a roller coaster, you know what I mean. A roller coaster goes round and round and up and down. The round, round, up and down is what makes the customer get all excited. If the roller coaster were simply to do one big upside down turn and nothing else, the roller coaster ride would be over in a matter of seconds. And so it is with your customer.

Your message starts with the problem. The problem gets the customer's attention. Then the solution kicks in. To keep the customer's attention, you have to bring up more detailed information about the problem. That gets the client's attention all over again. And so it goes. The problem gets the heart rate up; the solution gets the heart rate down. (We even use this roller coaster effect in live presentations, workshops, sales letters—and if you noticed, it's all over the pages of this book).

When you bring up the problem, it's like the first turn on the roller coaster. They're excited. Then you bring up the solution. And like the people on the roller coaster, your clients have calmed down a bit. Now it's time your marketing message got the customer excited again and again—and yet again. This factor of getting the customer excited is caused by the 'problem'. Which means that the 'solution' is close at hand as well, to calm the customer down.

But what's the purpose of bringing up the 'problem' and 'solution' so many times? Remember the purpose of the 'problem' and 'solution'? It was meant to get your attention. But that attention—like in the case of the cop car—soon wavers. The roller coaster effect keeps that attention going, so that the customer continues to stay at full alert as you continue to deliver your message.

But you can overdo either the 'problem' or the 'solution'.
Bring in too many problems, and the customer feels overwhelmed and feels unable to respond. Bring in too many solutions and the customer feels too relaxed. He/She feels no urgency to buy your product/service right away. So it's a factor of 'too hot' or 'too cold', but then what's 'just right?'

Let's take an example of a likely conversation:
Yoga centre owner: We help new mums quickly get back their pre-baby figure.
Mum: *How do you do that?*
Yoga centre owner: We find that mums put on a lot of weight during their pregnancies (problem), and want to get those extra kilos off (solution). But it's not just getting the kilos off that's the issue. Getting back to strenuous exercise can be difficult, and lead to injury (problem). We help mums get back to their pre-baby figure with injury-free yoga especially designed for new mums. And this helps new mums get back their pre-baby figure (solution).

As you can clearly see from the example, the conversation between the new mum and the yoga centre owner was richer and more detailed. You could clearly see the roller coaster effect, and how it helped both parties. The yoga centre owner was able to drive home the importance of choosing yoga (over other forms of exercise), and the mum was able to evaluate her choices as well.

But what if the conversation went like this?:
Yoga centre owner: We help new mums quickly get back their pre-baby figure.
Mum: *How do you do that?*
Yoga centre owner: We have yoga classes for new mums.

The answer still works, doesn't it? The chances are that the targeting is so darned good that the mum may still show up for the classes. But by bringing the roller coaster effect into play, the decision has become compelling for both parties.

Would it be fair to say that the mum would now be ready to sign on the dotted line? Far from it.

All we've done so far, is get and keep the attention of the client. And all we've removed are three red bags. It's time to move to conversion phase.

And get the rest of the four bags off that conveyor belt.

Summary: The Trigger

- A trigger is simply the ability of a message to stand out and get your attention. A trigger instantly gets the attention of the brain. And when faced with the trigger, the brain–your brain or the client's brain–has very little option but to respond very predictably.

- The role of the trigger is to get your brain to respond with curiosity. And when the brain is curious, it asks predictable questions such as 'How do you do that?' or 'What do you mean by that?'

- It's quite easy to water down the trigger. And when you water down the trigger, you get the 'kiss of death.' The 'kiss of death' isn't always apparent, but if you haven't activated the trigger, you're sure to hear statements such as:
  1) That's nice
  2) Hmmm
  3) That's interesting.

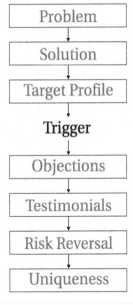

- The trigger does a great job of getting your audience interested. But interest alone is not enough. You need to keep their attention, so that you can get the next four bags off the conveyor belt as well. And so you've got to make sure the roller coaster effect comes into play.

- The roller coaster effect is simply the drama of bringing in the problem at regular intervals. Every time the problem pops up, the brain is reactivated and stays on full alert as you deliver your message.

- You shouldn't overdo either the 'problem' or the 'solution.' Roll out too many problems, and the customer feels overwhelmed and feels unable to respond. Bring in too many solutions and the customer gets too relaxed. He/She feels no urgency to buy your product/service right away.

The Objections

Why objections are gooooooooood!

Bag 4: The Objections

The moment we really want something to work, fear kicks in.

So if we're about to commit to a relationship, for instance, that's when the heebie-jeebies really starts to kick in. Our brains become a bit scrambled, as we work out the ramifications of our decision.

Should we go ahead? Shouldn't we? Should we?

We're confused, because our brain seems undecided.
One part of our brain wants us to go ahead.

Saying yes to anything means having to commit. And commitment brings its own headaches. Which is why fear kicks in immediately. Our brains scramble to find all the possible reasons where things can go wrong.

The other part of our brain is bringing up all the reasons why we should stay put. The very fact that we have to commit to the relationship causes us to come up with every reason why the relationship may not work—just so we can make it work.

Weird, eh?
But that's how our brains process information. When we take a decision, we want to prove to ourselves that we're not making a mistake. And the quickest mechanism our brains have to avoid making a mistake, is to put up a wall of objections.

And that wall of objections totally depends on the level of risk.
But you know that already, don't you? That you'd be plain silly to object like crazy when you're being sold a cup of tea, as compared with a $20,000 car. The level of risk ramps up the objections. The higher the risk factor, the more we object.

Or do we?
Actually we don't. We seem to have about six-seven main objections for pretty much every decision we make (And then just variations

of those six-seven objections). So yeah, if you think about it, you can quite easily come up with six-seven reasons why you shouldn't buy into a $2 cup of tea. Just as you could come up with six-seven reasons why you shouldn't be blowing $20,000 on a car.

But come on. Do we really have the same number of objections when the decision is trivial, as compared with a big decision like buying a house, or a car? Apparently size doesn't matter.

Let's take an example.
Let's say you have two free tickets to go see a movie. Let's say those tickets are valid until midnight tonight. Let's say the movie you want to see is running and there are seats available. And let's tip this totally in your favour, and throw in two packets of popcorn and two ice-cream cones as well. Are you ready to go?

You would think so, right?
You would think that if all the stars were aligned in favour of you going to the movies, you would be bolting out of that door. But incredible as it may seem, you're kinda putting up a wall of objections.

It's too rainy and cold to go out tonight.
But who'll take care of the kids?
The show's too late, and tomorrow's a work day.
There's not enough parking at the cinema.
We'll end up having dinner and blow the budget.
And yada, yada, yada.

Objections are not restricted to commitment alone. Even with a 'free pass to the movies', you are still able to come up with several reasons to stay home and watch reruns.

So it follows that even if you have the best product or service in the world, and if you have all your urgency factors in place, there's still going to be a decent amount of objections to whatever it is you're selling.

Of course, most of us wish these objections would just go away.
We so wish that the customer wouldn't be so nit-picky. And that the objections would just disappear. But they don't.

The objections don't go away, but it's important to recognise that objections are not a NO. They're just obstacles. Obstacles that need to be removed.

At no point has the customer said NO to the offering. Uh, huh! They could have said NO, and *that* would be *that*. But that's not *that*.

They're not saying NO.
They're saying, "Yes, I want to go to the movies, but can you remove these crazy obstacles?" And as you can see, our job when getting a point across, is to remove those crazy obstacles. So that the person taking the decision, is able to come up with their set of objections—and you in turn are able to logically overcome those objections.

Objections are not your enemy.
They are your friends. An objection literally means that the person who's doing the objecting, wants to take a decision to buy your product/service or idea. If they didn't care about the product/service, they'd just walk away.

In every commitment or purchase scenario, the 'buyer' is going to have objections. Hiding the objections doesn't speed up the 'sale,' because the objections don't go away in the 'buyer's' head. It's way better to bring up the objections and give each objection its due spotlight.

The fact that they're hanging around to object, means they're keen—at least at some level—to get you to convince them to buy the product/service. If someone is objecting, pay close attention. Because they are interested. Don't shoo them away. They're really the ones you should be focused on. Because they're going to tell you all the reasons they don't want to buy. And guess what? They've done all the hard work for you.

Now all you have to do is simply remove the objections, and you've removed one more bag: namely the objections.

Instead, most of us like to hide the objections.
Most of us secretly hope that the customer won't bring up any objections. That the customer will blindly buy the product or service.

And that's a silly hope.

Because we have objections for almost every transaction; everything we ever intend to buy will be peppered with at least a few objections. So why bother hiding the objections? Why not bring them to the fore instead?

Bring them to the fore? Won't that kill the sale?
Ah, *au contraire!* What will kill the sale is a stubborn attitude to try and hide the objections. When a customer is confused, or has questions that need to be answered, they don't usually pick up the phone and call you. They almost never email you or text you. Or send a carrier pigeon. They simply mull over the objection in their minds, and then they procrastinate.

The level of procrastination depends on the urgency.
If a customer needs to buy something right away, they will indeed call you; email you; text you; probably even turn up at your door.

And they'll voice their objections. And that's when you know you're missing something in your message.

You'll know that whatever questions the customer is asking haven't been answered. It's when you answer that question or objection, that the customer feels relaxed enough to go ahead with the decision.

Only a silly person would try and hide the objections in a sale.
Your customers are not two-year-old kids who accept your every word. As we grow up, we learn quickly that there are two sides to everything. Which brings us to two distinct facts.

Fact 1: That objections exist for every product/service.
Fact 2: That objections can't be hidden. And that if you're smart, you'll not only bring up the objections, but defuse the objections as well.

So how do you defuse the objections?
You defuse the objections by being prepared. You need to list out every possible objection that a customer could possibly ask. And you list the answer to those specific objections. If a customer comes up with more objections than you have on your list, just add it to that list of objections.

Drumming up a list of objections is like therapy. Once you know exactly what objections could possibly pop up in a transaction, you feel this huge sense of relief. Because now all you really have to do is defuse those objections. But remember, make a list first!

Creating a list of objections is important.
In a face-to-face selling situation, a customer may have the ability to bring up the objections, and hey, you have the ability to give the answers—and hence defuse the objections. However, if your customer is looking at your page online, you have no such luxury. When you have a list of objections prepared, you can list those possible objections and then defuse them.

And listing objections isn't just a good practice online.
It's actually a good practice no matter what media you use for getting a message across. If you're presenting an idea from a podium, there are going to be objections. If you're writing an article or report, there are going to be objections. If you're sending out an email, yes indeedy, there are going to be objections. And when you're selling something face to face, by golly, there are going to be objections.

So why not put the customer out of his/her misery and take a proactive approach? Why not bring up the objections in advance? And then why not defuse each objection one by one?

In fact, as you're bringing up the objections, you'll notice the customer nodding. Yes, they'll nod and they'll agree with you—or ask further questions. And the reason they're asking further questions, is because they want to be sure of the product/service they're buying.

But there's another subtle reason why the customer has so many objections.

The reason that we almost never consider, is that every sale is usually ratified by two people. So if a person buys a product or service, they'll almost always go back and talk to their partner, husband, wife, accountant, boss, colleague, friend, etc. Most of us like to make sure we've got a second opinion. And even though the other person may simply shrug and have no opinion, there's always the outside chance that the other person will have an objection. The other person will say something like: "But don't you think it's too expensive?"

And that's when we'll know if you've done your job well!
If you've anticipated and brought up all the main objections (even without the client prompting you) and then defused these objections, then here's what's going to happen. When your customer 'sells' the idea of a product/service to their partner/husband/wife etc., they'll be able to counter the objection of the partner/husband/wife etc. That's when you've really done a classic job. That's when you've literally got the customer 'selling' your product/service onwards. And in 'selling' the product/service onwards, they're now more committed to buying the product/service than ever before.

In most scenarios, you've got to overcome perceptions, and possible past experiences. And even then, the customer is likely to ask for a second opinion from their partner, accountant or see a review online. So any purchase goes through several filters.

But you may ask: 'If I wanted to find objections to my product/service, where would I start? And what if the product/service doesn't exist?'
Let's take one answer at a time. As far as starting goes, there are three core areas where objections pop up.

Your brain does strange yoga positions, long before you enter a yoga class. If you believe that yoga is all about flexibility, then that's a perception—not reality. And the perception is enough to prevent you from even considering yoga as a form of body and mind fitness.

1) **Perceptions**
2) **Past-Experiences**
3) **Need To Know.**

Perceptions are simply what we perceive to be true. It may or may not be true, but we don't really care. If we think it's going to be cold outside, and it's going to rain tonight, then well it's going to be cold and rainy. Unless of course, there's some evidence to the contrary. But in most situations the perception is the first reason why objections pop up.

The second reason why we object is based on past experiences. These may be our own past experiences, or someone else's past experiences. And as the saying goes, "Once burnt, twice shy". We're not that keen to go ahead and burn ourselves again, so we bring up the objections based on our personal history.

The third reason is just the unknown. When we're about to commit to something, we're not quite sure what we're getting into. We may have doubts that need to be resolved. These doubts aren't based on past experiences or perceptions. They're just based on a need to know the answers.

When dealing with the unknown, we're not happy campers. We get edgy, tentative and full of objections.

And to describe how this works in real life, let's take an example, and see how we use 'perceptions, past experiences, and a need to know' to create a nice bunch of objections.

Example: Yoga class

Perceptions: You may think you're not flexible enough. That you'll be the joker in the class. That the teacher may embarrass you. That you may have the wrong outfit. That the class may be just for advanced students.

Past Experiences: You may have not got adequate attention and injured yourself. You may have got too much attention, and been embarrassed. You may have felt the *asanas* were too complex.

Need to know: You may need to know if the yoga class is restricted to women. Or you may need to know whether the time and the schedule suits you.

As you can clearly see, we can bring up a reasonably long list of objections, simply by using the three categories of 'perceptions, past experiences and need to know'.

Provided of course, the product or service already exists.

But what if the product, service or idea doesn't already exist?
Or what if the customer hasn't had the chance to try out the product/service? What then?

But is your product, service or idea really brand new?
In many cases, it's a massive improvement over what's available in the marketplace, but there are still going to be perceptions and past experiences.

So if someone were to start up a 'Yoga on Ice' tomorrow, the customer would still need the reference point of yoga. If the customer hadn't run into the concept of yoga, you can still draw up a reference point of exercise, and how yoga is a form of exercise.

So no product, service or idea exists by itself. To explain a 'new' product, service or idea, you have to reference it to something that already exists. And as soon as you bring up something that already exists, you automatically bring in the perceptions, past experiences and the need to know.

In fact, if a product/service is too far ahead of its time, it's bound to fail.
Take parachutes for instance. The famous inventor/artist, Leonardo da Vinci, conceived an early version of a parachute hundreds of years before planes took to the air. The parachute was just too far ahead of its time, and hence Leonardo could logically defuse almost every objection, and still never be able to sell his idea to the public.

Which is why your product/service needs to build on other products/services in the market. And of course, when you build on existing products/services, you get similar 'perceptions' and 'past experiences' of those other products/services—and then some!

The buyer looks at your product or service and tries to find objections that are related to his/her own situation. The more you understand the objections, the more you can bring up the exact issues that most customers consider when buying into a product or service.

And here's how you can get a list of objections.
By sitting down and brainstorming all the possible objections within your sales force/staff. Or you can actually ask your customers/potential customers. The more you know, the more you're able to defuse objections and enable customers to buy products/services from you.

So let's vamoose back to our two recurring examples from the previous chapters and build on those examples.
Example 1: Website strategy workshop
Example 2: An allergy clinic

Website strategy workshop

Target Profile: Howard R.
Problem: *How do I grow my internet business, without compromising on my ethics?*
Solution: *Here's how to create a website strategy that's ethical, yet extremely profitable.*

Objections:
- *Not sure if I have time to implement more information*
- *Travel always takes time and energy*
- *I've just got myself a project manager which leaves me with fewer discretionary dollars*
- *Not sure if there's an overlap of information from other courses*
- *I don't need more tactics. What I need is a strategy.*

As you can see, we've got the problem, solution and target profile. And we've added the objections. If you do your target profiling exercise well, you'll get most—if not all—your objections from the person you choose to be your target profile. Now that we have Howard's objections, we can set about making sure we defuse those objections. The defusing of the objections is not a persuasion exercise. It's just a matter of explaining why his objections are not valid.

In effect once you've collated the objections, your next step is to highlight these objections in your marketing material or presentation. And then systematically defuse one objection after another.

An allergy clinic

Target Profile: Tricia M.
Problem: *How do I get rid of my allergic reaction to wine?*
Solution: *Here's how you can get rid of the allergic reaction in less than 24 hours (and without any pills or medication whatsoever).*

Objections:
- I've tried these anti-allergy clinics before and it didn't work for me
- The treatment seems to be quite expensive
- Will I have to go for several treatments on a recurring basis?
- What if the treatment doesn't work for me?
- How do I know that the person treating me is qualified?

Once again in Tricia's case, we can clearly see that despite the discomfort of the allergy, she's not completely convinced that the allergy clinic is the best solution. These objections come from past experiences of having tried to get rid of the allergy and not succeeding. And of course, the need to know factor. She needs to know if she's dealing with a qualified professional, or if there's a guarantee if the treatment doesn't work as advertised.

It's important to note that in most instances, the customer is keen to buy into the idea, service or product. Yet, they tend to hesitate. This hesitation is natural, and it's important that you answer the objections in great detail and never rush a customer through.

A rushed customer is a confused customer.
When pressurised, they may buy into your product, service or idea, but later regret their decision. This regret is one of the reasons why they return products, or ask for their money back. Even in situations where they don't ask for an exchange or a refund, they remember the experience of being rushed. And a rushed customer's brain embeds a memory of the pressure, and becomes hesitant to come back in future to buy more from you.

Your short term gain, leads to a long term loss.
The process of bringing up and defusing objections is a vital part of getting the customer calm and relaxed. It's when you present the objections and defuse them one by one, that you allow the customer to go ahead with their decision-making process. The pressure hasn't gone away. There's still a decision to be made by the customer. But the pressure isn't coming from the uncertainty. The

pressure switches to the customer, because now they're headed into a zone, where they're close to making a commitment.

And it's at this point, they start looking around for proof. They've listened carefully to what you have to say, but now want third-party proof. They want to hear, read or see instances where other customers went through the same decision-making process. And how other customers benefited from the commitment.

Your customers are looking for the 'testimonial bag'.

And here's what you need to pay close attention to: objections are the flip side of testimonials. I'll say it again. The objections form 'one side of the coin', and the testimonials are the 'other side of the coin.'

But why is this relationship between objections and testimonials so important to understand? You'll know in a short while, as we pick up Bag No. 5 from the conveyor belt.

Summary: The Objections

- The Objection is a big signal that the customer is interested. Disinterested customers don't object, or ask questions. They simply walk away. It's when customers are interested, that they feel the risk, that they start asking questions and objecting.

- Most of us hate when customers bring up objections. We treat objections like something we could do without. Yet, it's important to avoid hiding the objections. Instead of hiding objections, it's important to bring up the objections. When you do bring them up, you'll see the customer nodding in agreement.

- It's not enough to just bring up the objections, of course. It's pretty important to defuse the objections. And you defuse objections by coming up with a simple, logical answer for the likely objection. Every objection can be easily answered, provided you're prepared in advance. The worst thing that can happen, is that a client brings up an objection, e.g. your price is too high, and you sit there wondering what to say. [1]

- Objections can quite easily be split up into three main categories: perceptions, past experiences and need to know.

---

[1] Stumped while answering an objection? Go to http://www.brainaudit.com/objections to understand how to deal with objections—and more importantly, what NOT to say when answering an objection.

- Most of your existing customers as well as new customers will happily assist you in coming up with your list of objections—and often tell you how they'd want the objection dealt with as well.

- Objections and testimonials go hand in hand. They're intrinsically linked to each other. Objections are one side of the coin. And testimonials are the other side. Understanding the objections, leads to an understanding of what kind of testimonials you need to have in your message.

Testimonials

Why should I trust your goody-goody testimonials?

Bag 5: The Testimonials

You've seen résumés haven't you?
And what's common with all the résumés on the planet? Yup, they're all created to make the candidate look wonderful. Yet what's the first thing a company does when you present them with a résumé?

They check on the résumé details , don't they?
They go back and do some digging, and the smarter the company, and the more important the job, the more the company digs.

So you have to ask yourself: Why does the company check back on the résumé? And the obvious answer is: The company checks back, because they want to see the complete picture. They don't want the one-sided résumé view.

Most testimonials are made of sugar and spice, and everything nice. Which makes them not-so-reliable, because there are always two sides to a story.

And testimonials are like résumés: One-sided.
Most testimonials resemble résumés: They're all sugary. No matter where you look, testimonials are stuffed with wonderful adjectives, and powerful verbs. Every testimonial seems to talk about the 'magnificent, outstanding, and amazing' qualities of the product or service.

And after you've read a couple of those icky-sweet testimonials, you feel like you've had quite enough. If you had a big dose of wonderful testimonials, you start feeling a little sick.

And there's a reason why.

You're getting a massive overdose of 'sugar'. Those testimonials are so sucrose-laden that there's no way on earth that you're going to believe in them.

So what would it take to make a testimonial believable?
Just like a résumé needs both sides of the picture, so does a testimonial.

When we're considering a purchase, we feel out of our depth. We feel we somehow need some reassurance. And testimonials, sugary as they are, reassure us somewhat. But what if you had a more believable testimonial? A testimonial that not only shows us the 'after' scenario, but reveals the 'before' as well. A testimonial with the complete picture.

Presenting the 'reverse testimonial!'
So what's a reverse testimonial? A reverse testimonial is simply a testimonial that starts off in reverse. All testimonials start off with the praise, and continue with the praise of a product/service.

A reverse testimonial talks about doubt. It starts with the skepticism first. It describes the fear or uncertainty racing through the customer's mind at the point of purchase.

A reverse testimonial works because it speaks to us, in the way we speak to each other. When we're recommending a restaurant, or a movie to a friend or a colleague, we intrinsically lace our recommendations with doubt.

We say things like: "You know that seedy-looking restaurant, and how you don't really feel like going inside? They've got the most amazing food." Or we say things like: "You know that fancy looking restaurant that you think may be over-priced? Well we went there last night, and we had the most delicious food, and the bill was far, far less than we expected."

We tend to coat our testimony with at least a little bit of doubt.
And when a testimonial highlights these doubts first—yes first— they make the testimonial real. And believable. They give the testimonial power and depth. And make it less like a bunch of words strung together, and more like a story. And stories don't just fall into place. Stories have to be constructed.

So while you've probably got quite a few testimonials from your customers in the past, you've probably never 'constructed' a testimonial before. So instead of 'getting a testimonial', it's important to 'construct a testimonial' instead.

So what does 'construction of a testimonial' mean?
It doesn't mean fabrication. It doesn't mean you're going to make up some fake testimonials. Construction means you're using structure to get your testimonial. When you use structure, you don't get random testimonials, but instead get testimonials that are specific and story-like.

But how on earth are you going to create testimonials that have specific details and read like stories? In the past, you've tried to get testimonials from clients, but it always seems like they're procrastinating.

The reason why clients promise to write you a testimonial and don't do so, is because they're lost for words.

You don't want to 'get' a testimonial. You want to have a plan, so you can 'construct' the testimonial in a systematic manner instead.

They don't have specific parameters, and so when they sit down to write, they stare at a blank screen. And then they either write something that's kinda boring, sugary, or instead they just put off the writing for another day.

And there's a second reason too. Often, we ask for testimonials days, weeks, sometimes even months after the client has made the purchase. This time-delay makes it harder for a client to recall facts and results.

We have to make it easier for a client to give us a testimonial. And easily the best way to get a pretty detailed testimonial, is to ask six core questions.

The six questions you need to ask to get a powerful testimonial are:

1) What was the obstacle that would have prevented you from buying this product/service?
2) What did you find as a result of buying this product/service?
3) What specific feature did you like most about this product/service?
4) What would be three other benefits about this product/service?
5) Would you recommend this product/service? If so, why?
6) Is there anything you'd like to add?

There are six questions you need to ask to get outstanding reverse testimonials. Not only do you get great believable testimonials, but each testimonial is rich with emotion and detail.

And here's the explanation for each of those questions above:

1) What was the obstacle in your mind that would have prevented you from buying this product/service?
We ask this question because the customer always has a perception or an obstacle. No matter how ready the customer is to buy your product/service, there's always a hitch. The hitch could be money, or time, or availability, or relevance—or a whole bunch of issues.

And when you ask this question, it brings out those issues. And it does something more. It gives you an insight into issues you may not have considered, because the client is now reaching into their memory to see what could have been the deal-breaker.

And there's always an obstacle; always something you may not have considered. So when the customer brings up this obstacle, it presents an angle that's unique, personal and dramatic.

2) What did you find as a result of buying this product/service?
This question is important, because it defuses that obstacle. When a client answers this question, they are clear about why the purchase was worth it, despite the obvious obstacles.

3) What specific feature did you like most about this product/service?
Now you're digging deeper. If you ask the customer to focus on the entire product/service, the answer gets waffly. It's therefore important to focus on one feature/benefit that the customer liked most about the product/service. This brings out that one feature in explicit richness and detail.

4) What would be three other benefits about this product/service?
Having already got one big feature, you can now go a little wide, and see what else the customer found useful. You can substitute the word 'three' with 'two' or simply remove the number. The number allows the customer to focus on 'two' or 'three' things, and then give you those 'two' or 'three' things that were useful.

5) Would you recommend this product/service? If so, why?
You may not think this is an important question, but psychologically it's very important. When a customer recommends something, there's more than your product/service at stake. The customer's integrity is at stake too. So unless the customer feels strongly about the product/service, they won't be so keen to recommend it. And when they do recommend it, they're saying to prospective buyers: "Hey, I recommend it, and here are the reasons!"

6) Is there anything you'd like to add?
By this point, the customer has said all he/she has to say. But there's never any harm in asking this question. The questions before this question kinda 'warm up' the customer, and sometimes you get the most amazing parting statements, that you simply can't imagine. [1]

---

[1] If you ask these questions via email or via a medium where the customer has to type or write the answers, you'll get a much shorter, terser response. If on the other hand, you call up the customer and record the testimonial, you could be speaking for a good 15-20 minutes. And because we speak faster than we type, there's a far more conversational tone to the testimonial. Plus you can get a clarification, or more detail when you're speaking. Of course, all this recording is child's play via Skype or other recording devices (Check your local electronics store or go online to see how to 'record a phone call').

To see a simple tutorial on how to use Skype or other methods of recording calls, go to www.brainaudit.com/skype

And this detailed construction of testimonials brings us to a very interesting observation. That in fact, the testimonial is the flip side of the objection.

Notice the first question we asked the customer?: *1) What was the obstacle in your mind that would have prevented you from buying this product/service?*

And that 'obstacle' the customer is talking about is really their 'biggest objection.' So what does this tell us about how we should plan our testimonials?

We should plan our testimonials to directly defuse each objection.
So let's say you're keen to sell a trip to the wildlife on the Galápagos Islands. Obviously, the trip is an exciting idea for travellers seeking to explore the wildlife on the islands. But even thrill seekers will most certainly have their objections. So if you did your homework and interviewed the potential customer you'd get objections such as:

What's the biggest objection? Don't always assume it's price. It could be a fear of aliens, you know!

1) It's too expensive
2) It's too far to travel
3) There's no comfortable accommodation.

Now let's assume these are the three main objections.
What are the testimonials going to say?
1) I thought it was too expensive, but (here's what I found)
2) I thought it was too far to travel, but (here's what I found)
3) I thought we'd have to rough it out, but (here's what I found).

Each of the testimonials are mirror-images of the objections.

Sure you have already defused the objections earlier in your message, but this defusing is now being done by the customer, who is a third party. And you know what that means, right?

A third party is always far more believable to your prospective customers. And because each testimonial is specifically linked to an objection, it systematically reduces the risk not once, but twice.

But how do you go about controlling the angle of the testimonial?
You may want the customer to talk about expense, or distance travelled, or relevance. And the customer may want to talk about 'an overdose of workshops.' So how do you control the angle?

You don't. You're in the business of helping the construction of the testimonial. This means you're giving the testimonial structure. You don't need to control the situation. So here's how you go about attempting to get the angle you desire.

Mirror, mirror on the wall... what's the biggest objection of them all?

Let's say you have three main objections that you need to defuse.
And let's say you call up the customer. Ask the customer if 'expense, or distance, or comfort' was one of their big issues. If they say yes, continue down that track, and they'll give you the specifics of why 'expense' or 'distance' or 'comfortable accommodation' was an issue. But if they disagree, and come up with a completely different issue, e.g. they say, 'I thought the bad weather was going to be a dampener', then hey, keep following that customer's train of thought.

Because that train of thought is now revealing an objection you hadn't considered. It's talking about something you hadn't considered. And it may be a valid objection that hasn't come up before.

However, you may decide that the stray objection isn't worth pursuing. And that you can't use the objection and corresponding testimonial. Well, no problem. If you decide you can't use the testimonial, you can always call other clients to get the angle you're looking for.

Sooner, rather than later, you're going to get the exact objections, and the exact testimonials, that help to defuse those objections.

Which means that the testimonial isn't some-thing we just throw into our marketing. It means the testimonial is doing some real grunt-work in defusing objections. The factor that makes the testimonial so much more powerful, is that it's doing so from a 'third party' perspective, and doing it in a way that the seller could never do.

A testimonial angle is like one flavour of ice-cream on your ice-cream cone. It's best if you stick to one angle, instead of tackling too many. One angle allows the prospect to focus on just one aspect of proof.

You could never bring out the detailed specifics that a client brings out.
You could never paint the imagery and the emotion. And even if you could, it would sound like a whole lot of puffery. But when the client comes up with all that detail and emotion, the testimonial becomes rich, complex, but mostly very believable. And that's the main job of the testimonial.

Which brings us back to our two recurring examples. Let's see how we can use the testimonial in the examples.
Example 1: Website strategy workshop
Example 2: An allergy clinic

Each product or service has many testimonial angles. Make sure you use several angles in your testimonials.

Website strategy workshop

Target Profile: Howard R.
Problem: *How do I grow my internet business, without compromising on my ethics?*
Solution: *Here's how to create a website strategy that's ethical, yet extremely profitable.*

Objections:
- *Not sure if I have time to implement more information*
- *Travel always takes time and energy*
- *I've just got myself a project manager which leaves me with fewer discretionary dollars*
- *Not sure if there's an overlap of information from other courses*
- *I don't need more tactics. What I need is a strategy.*

Testimonial:
"I figured the Website workshop would be a rehashing of older material."

Before the Website workshop, I had my doubts about what I could learn. I have been on 5000bc for more than a year, read The Brain Audit - I'm even in the Protégé program. So I was a little skeptical about hearing anything new; I figured it'd be a rehashing of older material.

I also didn't know how I would swing the time away - I've been so busy implementing the Protégé teachings, and I was concerned that this might take me off-target.

And here's what I found:
I don't think I can really put into words how comprehensive and integrative the class was. We learned amazing material. We learned how to apply it to our businesses. We discussed and shared with others, so it wasn't just direct learning, it was tangential - we were 'cross-pollinated' by everyone else's epiphanies, so the learning was exponential. It was pretty darn amazing![2]

An allergy clinic

Target Profile: Tricia M.
Problem: *How do I get rid of my allergic reaction to wine?*
Solution: *Here's how you can get rid of the allergic reaction in less than 24 hours (and without any pills or medication whatsoever).*

Objections:
- *I've tried these anti-allergy clinics before and it didn't work for me*
- *The treatment seems to be quite expensive*
- *Will I have to go for several treatments on a recurring basis?*
- *What if the treatment doesn't work for me?*

Testimonial:
"I thought the treatment would be quite expensive. And I was right!"

The treatment was quite expensive. But was it worth the expense? Let's see. I've had this allergy for well over twelve years. And no matter what I did to get rid of the allergy, nothing seemed to work. In fact, when I really think about it, I may have spent far more money popping some kind of anti-allergy pills that only brought me temporary relief.

And here's what I found:
The allergy clinic treatment on the other hand, worked like magic. It's been six months since I've sneezed. And I can tell you I've been enjoying my red wine. I no longer have to rush home early with my face all puffy and red-eyed. I can stay and enjoy the company of my friends. And of course, when my husband and I spend a romantic dinner, I can enjoy a glass or two of fine wine, and the evening doesn't end up with me having to drink tomato juice instead!

---

[2] This is an excerpt from a 'mile-long' testimonial. It's a real testimonial given at a Psycho-tactics workshop, and is just one of many. Of course the workshop itself has to deliver the goods to get a testimonial. However as you read through the testimonial, you'll recognise the questions that were asked. And how that created a very comprehensive testimonial. To see examples of deconstructed testimonials, go to: www.brainaudit.com/testimonials

As you can quite clearly see, the objection plays a critical role in developing a testimonial that's not only rich in detail, but is extremely relevant to the potential customer.

Testimonials don't exist to do the rah-rah.
They're not there to make your page look sweet and sugary. The job of testimonials is to reduce the customer's fear of buying the product or service. They're there to build trust. They're there to make your product and service believable. And when testimonials are structured correctly, that's exactly what they do: they reduce risk.

And talking about risk actually takes us to the sixth bag: Risk Reversal.

Summary: The Testimonial

- Testimonials are like résumés; they're not entirely believable. Which is why most customers tend to view testimonials skeptically. Even if we don't say it out loud, we view testimonials as one-sided.

- It's the seeming lack of reality in a testimonial that makes us doubt its genuineness. So the way to pump back the reality is to give a testimonial a before/after effect. And voilà, we get the 'reverse testimonial'.

- The 'reverse testimonial' is nothing but a testimonial that brings to the fore how the customer was feeling before they made the purchase. The doubts; the slight discomfort; the pain; the frustration. These all run through a customer's mind right before they buy a product/service. These doubts need to be brought up front, because they bring a massive dose of reality to the testimonial.

- To get this factor of reality, we need to 'construct' our testimonials, instead of just 'getting' testimonials. Construction doesn't mean you're faking a testimonial. Construction means you're using parameters to build a structurally sound testimonial.

- It's not just a matter of asking the questions to construct a testimonial. Testimonials play an important role in removing objections. Therefore the objections must be listed. And it's important to then get testimonials that defuse the core objections that stop your customer from buying your product/ service.

- This of course, doesn't mean that you don't accept a testimonial that's given by a customer. Hey, a testimonial is a gift. And sometimes you get the most incredibly powerful testimonials from customers. Sure they may not have the awesome structure you're hoping for, but these testimonials still work. So don't go about being uppity and rejecting testimonials that don't fit the structure of the 'reverse testimonial'.

- Testimonials tell stories. Stories rich in colour and detail. Stories that you could not have dreamed up in a squillion years. And yet, these stories are totally believable, because they come from the customer. And more importantly, because they have a solid dose of reality at their very core.

Risk Reversal

Will it come back to bite me on the bum?

Bag 6: The Risk Reversal

One of my most favourite dishes in the world is a rice-dish called *biriyani*.

And so there I am sitting at an Indian restaurant we used to frequent almost weekly. At which point, the owner comes up to me and says he's got something special. Something that's not on the menu. Ok, no prizes for guessing, but yeah it was a *biriyani*.

Now I want you to get into my brain for a second, and think what I was thinking. So here's what I was thinking. They'll bring the *biriyani*. Of course, it will be too hot and spicy. So I'll complain. Then they'll take it back to the kitchen, and water it down with some yoghurty kind of mixture. And I'll hate it even more.

Do I want my money back? No, I most certainly don't! I want my biriyani back. And preferably without the extra chilli!

You see that's not what my brain is thinking about at all.
Instead I'm all ready with a big smile, and waiting in great anticipation for my dinner. But guess what happens next?

Yes, it was too hot and spicy (even for me). And yes, they took it back into the kitchen. And like some bad dream, they brought it back watered down with some yoghurty type of mixture, that made the *biriyani* absolutely horrid. And predictably, the restaurant owner comes up to me and asks if the *biriyani* is to my liking?

Of course it's not.
So guess what he does. He's hurt. He's confused. And the words that come out of his mouth are: "Oh, that's too bad. I guess I won't recommend any dishes to you in future."

Can you believe that statement?
You don't believe it, do you? Well neither did I. I wanted to scream at him. I wanted to say: "You dope! I'm not here to ask for my money back. I'm here to spend my money. I'm here to have a wonderful dinner—that's why I'm here. I don't want my money back. I want to get what I paid for. I wanted you to make the finest *biriyani* in the world, and I wanted to show up twice-a-week, instead of just once-a-week, to eat this fabulous dish."

Decaf: Check!
Soy: Check!
Latte: Check!

And yet, it would be nice to have my money back. And hey it's fair isn't it? I don't care if I spend $2 or $2000. When you spend your hard-earned money, you expect to get what you ordered. And if you ordered a decaf-soy-latte, you expect it to be decaf, and soy, and a latte. So if they can't provide you with the goods, then hey, they should—at the very least—make up for the gaffe. And ideally have a risk reversal policy in place.

Like the company Granite Rock has, for instance.
Now you may never have the need to buy concrete, sand or asphalt, but let's imagine you actually needed the stuff. And because you're a construction company dealing with a rock company, you're not overly impressed with all this marketing stuff. You want your concrete, your sand, etc. You couldn't care a hoot about any risk reversal policy.

So let's say you did decide to work with Granite Rock. And at the end of the transaction, you got an invoice. Nothing different about the invoice, except a few lines at the bottom that state: "If you are not satisfied for any reason, don't pay us for it. Simply scratch out the line item, write a brief note about the problem, and return a copy of this invoice along with your cheque for the balance."[1]

[1] I first read about this company in 'Good To Great' by Jim Collins. It's a book I'd very strongly recommend, because it goes deep into what makes companies (and individuals) great. And more importantly, it compares greatness, with not-so-great. It compares two companies facing the same opportunities; the same hurdles and the story of how one went on to greatness, while the other company fizzled like a two-day-old soda. Read it. As I said, I recommend it.

Notice something. It isn't a money-back policy. You don't have to complain. You don't have to do the rhumba to get your money back. You simply scratch out the item on the invoice, and send in the balance.

Now hey, it sounds like a nice story, right?
All warm and fuzzy, but surely this company must now be out of business. Quite the contrary. To quote Jim's research: [2] *"The little company—it has only 610 employees—has consistently gained market share in a commodity business dominated by behemoths, all while charging a 6% price premium.*

It won the prestigious Malcolm Baldrige National Quality Award in 1992. And its financial performance has significantly improved— from razor-thin margins to profit ratios that rival companies like Hewlett-Packard, which has a pretax return of roughly 10%."

And I would have paid a 6% premium for that biriyani.
I would have most certainly given the chef an award.
I would be most happy to drive every one of my friends, relatives and customers to that restaurant, from now 'til the gas prices no longer make it feasible to drive long distances.

All it would take is a little risk reversal.
Yet the restaurant had no such policy. And most businesses on the planet have no such policy either. They expect their customers to take on all the risk. Yet when the tables are turned, and they become customers, they fully expect to get what they paid for—and a little more on top.

So how do we go about constructing a risk reversal policy?
There are two stages to creating risk reversal.

1) The obvious risk
2) The hidden risk.

[2] Quote from Jim's website: http://www.jimcollins.com/lib/articles/07_99_b.html

The obvious risk: This is obvious, because it simply accepts that there may be a flaw in the product or the service. Or that the product or the service is not suitable to the customer's specific needs. So either the customer needs to test out the product/service in advance e.g. Test-drive the car; try before you buy. Or there's a flaw in the product/service, and there's a straightforward money-back guarantee or warranty.

Decaf: Check again!
Soy: Check again!
Latte: Check again!

Most companies do fine with this simple policy of reversing the obvious risk. If you take the Tilley Hat for example, you'll find this simple guarantee: "*Tilleys are replaced free if they ever wear out, shrink or fall apart. They're so carefully handcrafted in Canada, and made of such strong materials, that many outlive their owners.*"

Now replacement or warranties are pretty darned obvious, but is there a hidden risk? Is there some sort of risk that's almost sub-conscious? Yes, indeed, such a risk exists. It's the real risk. The risk that's never voiced. Never thought of.

And yet, when presented to the customer, this risk is the factor that causes the customer's eyes to light up.

Elephants can sit on it, dogs can chew it, alligators can chomp it. And Tilley guarantees it!

So let's look at the Tilley Hat again, and see if they have a hidden risk factor in place. And guess what? They do! Here's the hidden risk: Hats blow off in gusty conditions. Dogs find them irresistible; blackbirds find they make a good base for a nest.

And so Tilley fixes this problem with a simple statement:
INSURED AGAINST LOSS:
We understand the anguish of losing this reliable companion, or of having your dog

terminally gnaw it. Should that happen, Tilley will replace your late, lamented Tilley at half the catalogue price.

With your Hat, you'll be provided with "The Straight-Shooter's Statement of Loss of a Tilley Hat" insurance policy. The insurance is for two years, all perils, 50% deductible, and is not issued by Lloyds.

And suddenly, not only is the hat almost kryptonite-proof (it doesn't shrink, and it doesn't mildew, and it floats, and is waterproof) but it also covers the hidden risk: The risk of losing the hat.

Now tell me: If you wanted to buy a Tilley-like hat, what would you prefer? Just the usual yada-yada warranty? Or would you prefer the hidden risk to be covered as well.

At Psychotactics we've created the 'Lawn Mower Guarantee' for our home study products. This means you can return a product in any condition (even if you've run the mower over the product).

But the hidden risk is called the hidden risk, because it's, um, hidden. So to understand what the customer is really thinking, you have to dig deep. So let's take another example, shall we? And let's stick to Psychotactics.com this time.

Let's say you wanted to buy a self-study course...
And you were going to order all the CDs/DVDs and manuals. Well think about it: What's the obvious risk? The obvious risk is that having spent the money, you'll find that the product was either not to your liking, or not suitable for your needs. And for that, there's a 100% money-back guarantee. But is that enough? What about the hidden risk? But what could be the hidden risk?

Put yourself in the customer's shoes and it's not hard to find the hidden risk. Now some of us will tear open a package with our teeth, but what if you're a reluctant customer. What if you weren't 100% sure the product would suit your needs? Would you be slightly careful not to damage the product? You would, because in the past, you've been told: We'll take the product back, provided it's in the original packaging and in original condition.

But what if you got the 'Lawn Mower Guarantee'?
So what's the Lawn Mower Guarantee? *Here's the quote from the Psychotactics website: You get our 'Lawn Mower Guarantee'. Which means that if you decide all this information is rubbish, you can literally run your lawn mower over the material and we'll still give you all your money back. With no questions asked. Return it within 60 days for a complete refund. Just put it in a box (the home study, not the lawn mower ;) and send it back. And I'll be happy to refund your money with a smile."*

So, not only do you get the usual 100% money-back guarantee. But the hidden factor comes to the fore as well. With the hidden guarantee, you're now assured that you don't have to keep the product in its original condition. So guess what? Your hesitancy goes away. But where does it go away? After you've bought the product? No, not at that point. It goes away before you've bought the product. When you're reading the sales page itself, you get the feeling that you can get a refund no matter what.

But you needn't restrict yourself to one hidden guarantee. Because there may be more than one. So we have two. The second one is the 'Ask Anyone Guarantee'.

And again, here's the straight quote from the website: *The 'Ask Anyone Guarantee': Before you buy, if you want to speak to any of the participants/past clients, we can provide you with a list. You don't speak to whom we decide. You speak to anyone who attended/or bought this product/used this service. You pick the person from the list, and decide whom you want to call to find out if the product/service is worth the money. We had participants from*

The guarantee isn't some orphan. Give the guarantee some detail and hey, give it a name too!

Australia, New Zealand, Canada, Korea, quite a few countries in Europe, and the US. So you've got a wide range of people you can call.

Which brings us to another pertinent point: Naming the guarantee.
If you're going to take all the trouble to dig up the hidden risk, then you may as well give the risk reversal a name.

The branded risk reversal doesn't always work across all products and services. Handle each naming separately, as you would with any branding exercise.

Tilley calls it the 'The Straight-Shooter's Statement of Loss'. At Psychotactics, the 'Lawn Mower Guarantee' is well-known. What I'm saying here, is give the risk reversal a brand name. Because it's way easier for a client to remember a guarantee with a name, than just the terms of the guarantee.

The name puts the hidden risk in the spotlight. Your customers are not idiots. They know a risk when they see one. And they'll recognise that you understand their fears and doubts, and have taken steps to rectify the problem, should it ever occur.

And of course, it's natural to get lazy.
You might come up with a really cool hidden risk, and come up with a powerful, well-branded risk reversal. And then you may offer this risk reversal across every product and service. And that's a bit of a mistake (We know, because we keep making it). The hidden risk may work well across all your products/services. And then again, it may not. So while a 'Lawn Mower Guarantee' works fine for self-study programs, it won't work at all if you were trying to get people to a workshop. And your customers aren't going to find solace in a 'Lawn Mower Guarantee', if they're buying pipes, or ball bearings, or consulting services, or concrete for that matter.

Which is why Granite Rock offers the option of 'Short-Pay'. It knows that 'Short-Pay' works fine across all their products. And when you really sit down and think about it, the real difference between 'Short-Pay', and 'The Straight-Shooter's Statement of Loss', and the 'Lawn Mower Guarantee' is that they're not different at all. They're specific to the situation, and the product/service. But at the very core, they do one solid task.

They identify and reduce the obvious risk. And then they go one step further and find the hidden risk. And remove one more barrier that could possibly prevent the customer from buying.

But all of these facts don't make you feel any better, do they? What if your customers do ask for their money back in hordes? How can you spend six months of your life working on a project, and then simply hand over the money? And won't risk reversal cheapen your product/service?

So let's tackle one question at a time:
1) What if your customers ask for their money back in hordes?
2) How do you reconcile the fact that you've put in time and effort? And that it's the hardest thing in the world to simply refund the money paid for services/or replace the product?
3) Does risk reversal cheapen your product/service?

So will your customers ask for their money back in hordes?
The answer is yes. This happens when a product is blatantly defective. You've seen this with products such as defective cars, or defective medicines. The company that provides the defective products loses several millions just recalling the products. Often the customer is blissfully unaware of the defect, but they recall the product

So yeah, you're afraid of customers asking for a refund. But the only reason why you should be afraid is if you've got a crappy product or service. If your 'boat' doesn't have holes then the 'sharks' don't matter.

anyway, knowing fully well that they're liable. And of course, it's cheaper than a billion-dollar law suit.

However, these recalls are the exception rather than the rule.
If your customers are going to ask for a refund in hordes, then you're essentially doing something wrong. And remember one thing: It's very, very hard for a customer to ask for their money back. Most customers will do nothing. They'll never buy from you again, but they'll almost never ask for their money back. So if you're getting a lot of customers complaining, it means your product is defective, and your service isn't doing what it's expected to do.

So it's a good thing if your customers are complaining. It's better to take the complaints on the chin, and fix the problems, than whine about the complaining customers. The only customers that do complain are those who want you to improve (remember the biriyani episode). The people who don't care about you won't complain, but will leave anyway.

Which brings us to the second question.
How do you reconcile the fact that you've put in time and effort? If you're in the product business, then it's hard enough to have to dig into your stock to replace a product. But if you're into services, it really is a matter of management. So let's take an example of how this may work for say a consulting firm, or a graphic designer or someone who's specifically doing a project.

You don't have to risk reverse your entire project. You can cut up a project into slices (pretty much like a cake). And risk reverse each slice. That way you're only taking a limited risk.

Every project can be broken up into several sub-projects.
Think of a project as a cake and you're cutting up slices. You can slice each sub-project so that it only involves a limited amount of work. That particular slice has an unconditional risk reversal. So keeping in mind that it's a thin slice, you complete the job, and if you haven't done it up to scratch, then you fix it, or the project stops moving ahead.

This step-by-step system does two things.
It reduces the risk of both the client as well as your risk. But it also allows you to invoice the client, and make sure the amount is paid for, before the project moves along. Yes, you've put in time and effort, but if you keep the project sliced really thin, you can reverse the risk every step of the way.

And the final question.
Will risk reversal cheapen your product/service? If you truly believe that you're doing the best for your customer, then shouldn't the customer make up their mind right at the start, whether to choose your offering?

And a risk reversal doesn't cheapen your product at all. In fact, as Jim Collins points out, it's a catalytic mechanism, that you must have in your system, because it enables you to spot faults—and iron them out quickly. If there's no risk reversal in place, complaints are just complaints that a company could possibly ignore. But when you offer a risk reversal and clients actually ask for their money back, you've got to move quickly to see that the problem doesn't reassert itself and cause more financial damage.

Risk reversal is a catalytic mechanism that helps you stay afloat rather than sink. Refunds are early warning systems. Pay attention to them, and fix your products and services sooner than later.

Rather than cheapen your products/services, it says that you stand behind your offering. Because when a customer can quite plainly see that you believe in your product, they feel the risk slide away much faster.

And by this point, they're only asking one question: What makes your product/service unique?

Aha, time for the last bag: Uniqueness.

But before we go over to the final bag, let's take a look at the two examples we've been tracking right through this book.

Example 1: Website strategy workshop
Example 2: An allergy clinic

Website strategy workshop

Target Profile: Howard R.
Problem: *How do I grow my internet business, without compromising on my ethics?*
Solution: *Here's how to create a website strategy that's ethical, yet extremely profitable.*

Objections:
- *Not sure if I have time to implement more information*
- *Travel always takes time and energy*
- *I've just got myself a project manager which leaves me with fewer discretionary dollars*
- *Not sure if there's an overlap of information from other courses*
- *I don't need more tactics. What I need is a strategy.*

Testimonial:
"I figured the Website workshop would be a rehashing of older material."

Before the Website workshop, I had my doubts about what I could learn. I have been on 5000bc for more than a year, read The Brain Audit - I'm even in the Protégé program. So I was a little skeptical about hearing anything new; I figured it'd be a rehashing of older material.

I also didn't know how I would swing the time away - I've been so busy implementing the Protégé teachings, and I was concerned that this might take me off-target.

And here's what I found:
I don't think I can really put into words how comprehensive and integrative the class was. We learned amazing material. We learned

*how to apply it to our businesses. We discussed and shared with
others, so it wasn't just direct learning, it was tangential - we were
'cross-pollinated' by everyone else's epiphanies, so the learning was
exponential. It was pretty darn amazing!*

Risk Reversal:
*1) Money-Back Guarantee
2) Ask-Anyone Guarantee.*

An allergy clinic

Target Profile: Tricia M.
Problem: *How do I get rid of my allergic reaction to wine?*
Solution: *Here's how you can get rid of the allergic reaction in less
than 24 hours (and without any pills or medication whatsoever).*

Objections:
*- I've tried these anti-allergy clinics before and it didn't work for me
- The treatment seems to be quite expensive
- Will I have to go for several treatment on a recurring basis?
- What if the treatment doesn't work for me?*

Testimonial:
"I thought the treatment would be quite expensive. And I was right!"

*The treatment was quite expensive. But was it worth the expense?
Let's see. I've had this allergy for well over twelve years. And no
matter what I did to get rid of the allergy, nothing seemed to work.
In fact, when I really think about it, I may have spent far more
money popping some kind of anti-allergy pills that only brought me
temporary relief.*

And here's what I found:
The allergy clinic treatment on the other hand, worked like magic.

It's been six months since I've sneezed. And I can tell you I've been enjoying my red wine. I no longer have to rush home early with my face all puffy and red-eyed. I can stay and enjoy the company of my friends. And of course, when my husband and I spend a romantic dinner, I can enjoy a glass or two of fine wine, and the evening doesn't end up with me having to drink tomato juice instead!

Risk Reversal:
1) Testimonials of clients with similar issues
2) No pills or invasive techniques guarantee.

You'll notice a slight variation in the two risk reversal examples. The first risk reversal for the workshop is based on the factor of '100% Money-Back' and 'Can I Ask Anyone?' The allergy clinic on the other hand can't promise a result.

So while they have to stick to testimonials to provide proof, they can still bring up the hidden risk reversal and reduce the risk. Every step you take to reduce risk makes it easier for the client to take a more informed decision. And to choose you instead of some other supplier. So make sure you worked darned hard on that risk reversal.

Butter Chicken Recipe

By the time you get to this part of the book, you're sure to be hungry for some Indian food. Well here's a verrrrrry cool recipe for Butter Chicken. It's not the watery Butter Chicken you get at your food court, or at most Indian restaurants. Just a look at the ingredients will convince you that this isn't an ordinary dish at all. So try it. You'll love it!

Don't take my word for it. You'll be licking your fingers, dishes and everything else in sight after you're done.

If you've got an Indian store down the road, you can pick up most of these ingredients without a problem. I've even seen some of the supermarkets stock them. It's not a treasure hunt. Most of this stuff is easy to find.

Preparation Time: Expect to spend a couple of hours (at least!)
Serves: 4–6

Ingredients:
100gm cashew nuts (A handful)
1 kg fresh tomatoes or Puree
$^1/_4$ litre cream (Here come the calories!)
Boneless chicken 1–1.5 kg
Ginger $^1/_2$ inch piece
Garlic 1 pod
Yoghurt 200 gms (1 cup)
Salt (as per your high blood pressure … ☺)
9 onions (ha, ha, ha – you'll need these laughs when you cry)

Indian store purchase section:
Garam masala (available at the store)
1 tsp dried coriander + 1 tsp dried cumin powder
25 Kashmiri chillies (Red dried chillies). Discard the seeds and make a paste of the chillies by soaking them in water.

Step 1:
1) Marinate the chicken with garam masala, salt, yoghurt, and keep in the fridge overnight.

2) Chop the onions fine, and fry them in oil or ghee till brown. Add ginger and garlic paste and fry for some time. Add the Kashmiri chilly paste and cook for some time. Add the coriander and cumin powder and keep frying. Then add the garam masala and keep at it … tomato puree is next on the list and fry well till cooked. As a finale, add the cashew nut paste and cook till it thickens and then set aside.

Step 2:
Take the marinated chicken and lay the pieces in the oven tray greased with ghee or oil. Important – Don't use the liquid from the marinade while roasting. Set the liquid aside for later (This can also be done in a frying pan if you don't have an oven).

After the chicken is roasted, add the reserved liquid. Cook for some time. Finally add the cream and cook for 2 minutes. Set aside.

Smoking Section:
This is really cool and not to be missed!
Take a couple of pieces of charcoal. Heat the charcoal on a flame until they get really hot and glowing. Take these pieces and put them in a very small open vessel or small metal container. Warm 3-4 tbsps of oil and pour it over the glowing charcoal. The charcoal will immediately start to hiss and smoke.

Decaf: Check once more!
Soy: Check once more!
Latte: Check once more!

Then immediately immerse the vessel in the chicken dish (this is to give flavour, so make sure it doesn't get into the chicken itself. It needs to be on top like a boat on the ocean). Cover the main chicken dish vessel immediately to seal in the aroma.

After a while open the vessel. Remove the charcoal and your dish is ready to serve. Garnish with fresh coriander!

Summary: The Risk Reversal

- As a customer, you feel the spectre of risk when buying a product or service. But as soon as you become the person selling the product/service, you feel that the customer should be the one to take the risk. And that's erroneous thinking. For customers to even try the *biriyani*, they need to know that all the risk lies with the seller. This makes a customer far more willing to buy your product/service.

- Logically risk reversals should hamper growth and profits. But quite the opposite is true. Companies such as Granite Rock, not only charge more in a cut-throat market, but also make very healthy profits. Plus they get free publicity, which can't be harming their cause.

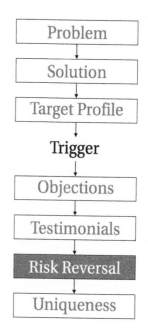

- There are two types of risk reversal. The obvious kind. And the hidden kind. You have to really get into the brain of the customer to work out the hidden risk. When you do find the hidden risk, you're getting at the core of what causes a customer not to buy—and removing that risk.

- You can't always take one type of hidden risk and run it across every product and service. A risk factor that works for one type of product, or one type of application, won't necessarily work for the next. So analyse the risk for each application. Being lazy and slapping one type of risk reversal across the board, isn't going to help you sell more products/services.

- Remember to name the risk reversal. It may seem like a trivial detail to you, but it's not. When customers want to reference the risk reversal, they're able to pull up a couple of words, instead of a long-winded risk reversal policy. Once they do have a branded risk reversal, they're able to quickly expand what the risk reversal stands for.

- You may believe that risk reversing is risky. But customers will only ask for their money back if your product/service really needs to be fixed. If you're working on a service-only project, break up the project into tiny slices, and give a risk reversal for each slice, only moving ahead when you've finished that slice of work.

- And finally, risk reversal doesn't cheapen your product. In fact, it makes your product way more desirable, because now both the obvious as well as the hidden risk has been reduced dramatically.

Uniqueness

Why should I buy from you?

Bag 7: The Uniqueness

There's a fundamental flaw in creating uniqueness.

And if you've ever had your picture taken, you'll know what I mean.

"Say cheese," says the person behind the camera.
And you say cheese. Your facial muscles are frozen. You have a dumb, goofy look. And under your breath you're muttering, "C'mon take the picture, take the picture, c'monnnn!"

Click! You blink. The picture's been taken.
And then the photographer runs across to you, all excited to show the nice digital photo. You take a look, you roll your eyes. You cringe. Because you just detest the photo.

It looks artificial. It looks posed. It's not you. It looks like all those 'cheesy' pictures you've seen before. It's not unique.

How can it be unique? You weren't yourself!
And that's the whole problem with uniqueness. You've tried too hard. In your business you've tried your darndest to get your own uniqueness. And you've failed miserably. Because you froze.

And the uniqueness you sought to find, looked like the cheesy picture in the third paragraph. When asked about your uniqueness, you mumble something like 'service or quality', which means nothing to most people.

The big problem with uniqueness is that you're trying to find your uniqueness. And you end up with some cheesy line. What you need to do is 'create your uniqueness.'

And this lack of uniqueness is a problem if you own a business.
Imagine you own a yoga centre. And a yoga centre is a yoga centre, right? So it's possible to twist your brain like a pretzel, and yet find it's almost impossible to come up with a form of uniqueness.

So naturally you'll do what all the experts recommended.
You'll ask your clients. And some of them will shrug, not knowing what
to answer. And some of them will give their glib answers like 'quality'
or 'service' or something that may seem helpful, but doesn't make
your class sound unique. And then there's a third set of clients who
will give you different reasons why you stand out, and what makes you
unique. Which means you now have a grocery list of unique points.
And not surprisingly, it confuses you more than ever before.

So you'll do what most businesses do. You'll choose something so
safe, that 'the uniqueness' is invisible. Or you'll just give up. At the
end of the day, a yoga centre is a yoga centre, is a yoga centre, right?

Wrong!

You know it and I know it. Your yoga centre is different, and it makes
no sense to stay a 'commodity' if you can stand out and be unique.
The only reason you've given up, or played safe is because of the
end result. The end result of this entire uniqueness exercise drives
you up the wall, and gives you no satisfaction.

So what if we change the technique? You see you could be going
about creating uniqueness in the wrong manner.

You're trying to find your uniqueness.
You don't need to find your uniqueness
at all. Because finding your uniqueness
assumes you've done something amazing
or fabulous in the past. But what if we
dropped the past completely? What if we
focused on the future instead?

Let me explain.

Most people trying to find their uniqueness
ask the question: What's unique about my
business? Instead they should be asking:

Choosing your
uniqueness is often a
big pain in the you-
know-where. How do you
choose?

"What do I *want to do* in my business that's different from everyone else?"

So let's go back to your yoga school. If you were asked: 'What's unique about your business?', you'd struggle to give an answer. But if you changed the question to: What would you want to achieve for your students most of all? Aha, that's a whole new question, isn't it?

Your brain now sees what it wants the clients to achieve. It seeks out the purpose. It brings out the specifics that eluded you before.

So let's say you started out at the yoga school to 'prevent injury in yoga', then when asked the question: 'What do you want to achieve for your clients/why did you set up this yoga school?', you come up with a completely different answer.

Your answer may be: "You can really hurt yourself in a yoga class if you're doing the wrong thing. I want every student to have Injury-Free Yoga."

You don't find your uniqueness; you invent it. Choose one of the factors you want to be the best at, and then build your business around that factor of uniqueness.

Tum..dee..dum. Can you see it? You can, can't you? Your uniqueness is *Injury-Free Yoga.* Plain and simple.

What's the one reason you set up your business?
What do you want to do, differently from everyone else?
What's your dream for your customer?

Ask Tom Monaghan, founder Dominos Pizza.
Today you take quick pizza delivery for granted. But if you zapped your way back to the swinging, hey-groovy seventies, you'd grow old just waiting for a pizza.

You'd call a pizza place. You'd ask, "Can you deliver?" And about seventy-nine hours later, you'd be still tapping your fingers waiting for the pizza guy to arrive.

Tom Monaghan knew this was a problem. That customers weren't angling for the best pizza in the world. That by the time the customer picked up the phone, they were already hungry. That the best thing to do was to create a uniqueness based not on the pizza, but on the speed of the pizza delivery.

Tom Monaghan literally invented his uniqueness.
He worked out how to get a pizza to his customer in 30 minutes or less. And then he came up with Dominos now historic slogan. 'Dominos Pizza. In 30 Minutes or It's Free!'

Are you getting the point?
You can't find uniqueness. It's easier trying to touch your tongue to your nose (Don't try that! I know you will ☺).

The uniqueness has to be invented.
Make it up.
Think of your wildest wish; your wildest dream and write it down.

And here's a good way to invent your uniqueness: You look at your business like you were a monarch surveying his kingdom. There you are at the top of the cliff looking down on your kingdom. And you want to create a kingdom like no other.

Your kingdom could be the safest kingdom.
Or the richest. Or have the best healthcare. Or be the most technologically advanced. Whatever you decide (and you have to decide) choose one factor.

One factor.
One.
As in not two.
Or three.

Yes, we know you can make three wishes.
Yes, we do know you're proficient enough to handle safety, and healthcare and technology and yada, yada. But let's not forget the purpose of this exercise. Uniqueness stands for 'one thing'.

Choose one.

Just like The Benjamin in New York.
The Benjamin—a hotel in Manhattan, New York—created a factor of uniqueness all by themselves. They decided that most business travellers needed a really good night's sleep above everything else.

But it's easy to argue against the thought process of The Benjamin. Because when you look at it, a good night's sleep is only one of many things a traveller needs.

Business travellers need superfast broadband connections; and food at ungodly hours; and great bathrooms, etc. There is a massive list that any hotel can draw up in a matter of seconds, that describes what most business travellers require when staying at the hotel.

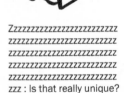

Zzzzzzzzzzzzzzzzzzzzzzzzzzz
zzzzzzzzzzzzzzzzzzzzzzzzzzz
zzzzzzzzzzzzzzzzzzzzzzzzzzz
zzzzzzzzzzzzzzzzzzzzzzzzzzz
zzzzzzzzzzzzzzzzzzzzzzzzzzz
zzz : Is that really unique?

But The Benjamin decided to focus on the sleep aspect. That's what uniqueness is all about. It's not about this and that, and that, and that. It's unique, remember? One thing. Just one thing. Yes, you're super-brilliant at many things, but it's time to choose one.

Because the advantages of choosing just one thing leads to several benefits:
1) You can make your company's offering simple and understandable
2) It becomes the DNA of your company. Everything revolves around that uniqueness

3) Your customers and the media start to see you as different and hence newsworthy.

So let's start with the newsworthy part and wind our way up. Let's take another look at The Benjamin. And let's see the review they got in the New York Times. And I quote:

The Benjamin Hotel in Midtown Manhattan helped invent the position of sleep concierge nearly seven years ago when its concierge staff noticed that more and more of their guest questions involved sleep. It is one of only a few hotels to offer the service, with the Fairmont in Washington and the SoHo Metropolitan Hotel in Toronto offering similar services.

Steps away from the No. 6 subway train and Lexington Avenue in full havoc, The Benjamin has deployed an array of anti-insomnia weapons.

They include guest rooms that begin on the fifth floor, high above street noise, with soundproof windows; luxury sheets; aromatherapy; massages; satin sleep masks; tips for "executive" naps; a menu of 11 special pillows, including the "Snore-No-More"; and special sleep-inducing foods, like banana bread with peanut butter.

The hotel, at 50th Street and Lexington, has a guarantee, said the sleep concierge, Anya Orlanska, who speaks with a slight Polish accent.

"You must sleep well or you will get your money back," she said.

Jennifer King, a technology consultant originally from Chicago, stayed at The Benjamin Hotel last month. She did so because Ms. Orlanska had done a deft job of finding a good hairdresser for Ms. King's mother when Ms. Orlanska was the concierge at the New York Palace Hotel.

Ms. King noticed the pillow menu and other offerings, but, she said, "I didn't think it was going to be that big of a deal."

That's not a food menu. It's a pillow menu. Surprised? Don't be. Because if you head to The Benjamin Hotel in New York, sleep comes first on the menu.

A sufferer of back pain, Ms. King said she had never been able to sleep for more than three hours a night without getting up.

But with a firm mattress and a special pillow — the "Swedish Memory," with self-molding foam developed by NASA — she was able to sleep for eight hours, she said. "And this was during the United Nations General Assembly and police escorts and traffic and people all around," Ms. King said. "I couldn't believe it."

And there's more…

At The Benjamin, Ms. Orlanska, 37, the hotel's senior concierge, said she advises dozens of guests a day on their sleep. She and the three other Benjamin concierges are trained in the sleep program, and spend the majority of their time dealing with sleep issues, while also doing the usual concierge duties like finding theater tickets to "Mary Poppins."

Three days before a guest is scheduled to arrive, the staff advises him or her of the pillow menu so that the pillow will be in the room when the guest arrives. The program is constantly expanding. A new iPod pillow plays music in the pillow itself.

Most of the pillows shift the body, usually on the side. The "Snore-No-More" elevates the chin. The maternity pillow eases stress on the abdomen.

Ms. Orlanska said she must often play psychiatrist to identify the causes of stress, like back-to-back meetings. A tip sheet, "Take an Executive Nap," which advises that a 60-minute nap is better than a 30-minute nap, usually does the trick. She'll also resort to banana bread.

Only one guest actually collected on the hotel's guarantee, said Eileen McGill, who was a concierge at The Benjamin for more than six years.

Consolidated Edison was jackhammering one night, said Ms. McGill, now the senior concierge at Manhattan House, a condominium complex on the Upper East Side.

"We gave him his money back," she said, even though he was only one out of several hundred guests who complained.

Now this brings us to the second point.
If you choose a uniqueness, then you can start to build your entire company around that one concept. If you were paying attention to the review, you'd have noticed that they solved a problem, bringing a solution to a very specific audience. They destroyed the high-price objections. They have testimonials that hark back to their uniqueness. And whaddya know: The risk reversal is also intrinsically linked to their uniqueness.

See, the entire core, the entire DNA of your company, can be built around one unique factor. Not two. Or three.

One.
Just one.

And to the third biggest reason why you need to drop everything and work out your uniqueness: You can make your company's offering simple and easy to understand.

So let's prove that point, shall we? What is The Benjamin in New York best known for? Aha, I don't have to prompt you, do I? You already know what to say. Because the uniqueness is drummed into your system. Just like Volvo

Volvo's uniqueness is safety. How did they get this uniqueness? They created it. And thus created a DNA for their products worldwide.

brings up the concept of 'safety' in your brain, The Benjamin must make you feel very, very sleepy.

Aha, but there's a problem here.

It's not enough to simply have a uniqueness. You need to tell the world about it.

If you go to the website at The Benjamin, you can't actually find their sleep guarantee (well, I searched, and I couldn't find it). And while the hotel is covered regularly in the press for their uniqueness, there's almost no mention of it on the website (where I'd look first, if I wanted to book a hotel).

To be fair, the website has been updated to reflect the fact that The Benjamin does sponsor the 'Great American Sleep Challenge' and the 'National Sleep Awarness Week'. But enamoured as I am with this hotel, I don't see the connection. I don't see the uniqueness, unless I actually was aware of the uniqueness in advance.

And this brings us to a very pertinent point.
It's not enough to have a uniqueness. It's critical to propagate the uniqueness everywhere. On your website, in your brochures, in your speeches, in your presentations and wherever you're sending out messages to your customers.

But how do we know if our customers are indeed receiving the message?
That's quite an easy answer actually. Ask a customer what Volvo stands for, and pop comes the answer. If your customer can't tell you the uniqueness of a brand in a millisecond, then either you don't have a uniqueness, or you've failed to make the uniqueness well known.

Sigh!
Deep sigh!

So many of us are afraid to stand out.
So many businesses lose customers and suffer the ignominy of ridiculous pricing, simply because they won't sit down and work out their uniqueness. And then having worked it out, they do nothing with it. Or worse, in an attempt to get a message across, they bring out several factors, and completely water down the message.

You see, The Benjamin may have the most delicious vegetarian meals in Manhattan. They may have a one-of-a-kind sparkling wine from Italy. They may have movie stars staying at their hotel. They may be really pet-friendly. They may have this and they may have that. And if they were to succumb to the temptation of trying to say it all, they'd simply water down the uniqueness.

It simply wouldn't be one thing.

But pray, how do you know that the one thing you've chosen works as well as it should? Well, we already know that you can ask your customer and gauge their response. But before you do get to the customer, you have to test it out yourself so that you don't end up with egg on your face. Because your uniqueness may not be so unique after all.

The logo test instantly tells you if your product is unique— or not.

So here's a little trick to find out if your uniqueness works.
Take the logo of your product or service. And slap your uniqueness under that logo. Now swap your logo with another company's logo. Does the uniqueness still work? It does, doesn't it?

You'll find it hard to admit, and you'll argue that your uniqueness is indeed unique. Then along comes the customer. And you ask them for the uniqueness, and guess what happens next? Yup, the customer stumbles, fumbles and you've got your proof.

The proof is that your uniqueness is unknown to the customer.
No one knows it, or understands it. But they do understand the uniqueness of Volvo and The Benjamin. And Volvo and The Benjamin must have had to do the same soul-searching to begin with. They too would have had the most frustrating, screaming board meetings. They too would have had their doubts.

It's when you bite the bullet and stand for one thing that you really create a uniqueness factor. And that uniqueness factor creates the basis for everything you do and say. Which when you think about it, is a big relief. Because no matter if you're an atom-sized business or a big business, there's a uniqueness waiting for you. There's always an angle that you haven't discovered.

And yes, you've understood that you need to work on your company's uniqueness, but you still resist. You find all the reasons to avoid going through this uniqueness exercise.

Somehow this uniqueness factor seems like too much hard work. And it is. But that's precisely why you should do the hard work. For one, it creates a sense of clarity of who you are. Your customers understand why they choose you instead of the competition. And because it's so much hard work, your competition will keep procrastinating, and give you a massive headstart, and even get some of your competitor's customers over to your side of the fence.

And there's one more big reason why you need to define your uniqueness sooner than later.

Imagine you took the six bags off the conveyor belt. Would you have done enough of the grunt-work? Technically yes. But if you don't remove the seventh bag—the bag called 'Uniqueness'—all you've really done is set up the customer to go to the competition.

You've given your customer lots of information, but without a factor of uniqueness, your product/service appears to be exactly like the next person's product/service.

You may not agree. You may say you're absolutely unique. That you're different in a lot of ways. But the customer isn't in your 'store' to listen to your rants. They want to know why they should buy from you. It's your job to make that uniqueness simple and dramatic enough.

So how do you go about creating a uniqueness factor for your company? You do it in steps.

Steps to The Uniqueness

Tah-dah, here are the steps you need to take to make your business unique.

Step 1: Make a big list of what makes your business unique
Step 2: Weighted ranking will help you decide on the most
       important reason
Step 3: Flesh out the uniqueness to create more clarity.

Step 1: Make a big list of what makes your business unique.
Sit down and brainstorm with others in your company. And if you're a tiny business, sit down and brainstorm with a friend, or some people who know you well. You may find a spouse or partner to be very helpful as well.

What's important when you're doing this brainstorming, is to write down everything—no matter how ridiculous it may sound. Just write down the list. Don't analyse.

Step 2: Use weighted ranking to decide.
Weighted ranking (see box on page 130) will help you decide what you consider to be the most important factor of uniqueness for your company. Using weighted ranking is effective, because it clearly shows a preference.

Step 3: Flesh out the uniqueness to create more clarity.
Now that you're clear what you'd like to be unique at, you need to bring more colour and detail to that uniqueness. It's not enough for you to understand what the unique factor is all about. It's important for the customer to know as well.

So let's find out how The Benjamin could have gone about this exercise [1]

[1] Note: The Benjamin is just an example. Psychotactics.com has no input into the development of their uniqueness (Just in case you were wondering).

What is weighted ranking?

Weighted ranking is used for more accurate decision-making. Usually when we're asked to make a decision, we're often asked to numerically rank a list in the order of importance. e.g. 10 is the least important, and 1 is the most important. This method is flawed, because it forces you to choose one over the other. So if you were given a choice between coffee, tea and hot chocolate, you may prefer hot chocolate on some days and tea on other days. And not drink coffee at all. But when forced to rank, then you may vote a tea over a hot chocolate. So your ranking may end up looking like this:

1- Tea
2- Hot chocolate
3- Coffee.

This is inaccurate, because you love hot chocolate as much as tea. And you don't like coffee at all. And hence the ranking above would be mostly inaccurate. However, if you use weighted ranking, you're responding to a question based on your preference. So if I were to give you ten votes, and tell you to allocate those votes between tea, coffee and hot chocolate, then the result may look like this:

Tea - 5 votes
Hot Chocolate - 5 votes
Coffee - 0 votes.

Suddenly there's a marked change in our understanding. This weighted ranking tells us that both tea and hot chocolate are equally desirable. And coffee is eeeyuck!

Of course we could just as easily end up with a result like this:

Tea - 7 Votes
Hot Chocolate - 3 Votes
Coffee - 0 Votes.

This shows our clear preference, and hence is more accurate than ranking a list numerically.

Weighted ranking really gets your brain churning. It forces you to choose based on your preference, instead of simply ranking what's important and what's not.

Step 1: Make a big list of what makes your business unique?
1) Super fast broadband access
2) Food at ungodly hours
3) Great bathrooms
4) Good night's sleep,

Step 2: Weighted ranking that could have ended up like this:
1) Super fast broadband access - 0 votes
2) Food at ungodly hours - 2 votes
3) Great bathrooms - 3 votes
4) Outstanding beds - 5 votes.

Now we have a clear winner.

Step 3: Flesh out the uniqueness to create more clarity.
This is where the concept is fleshed out. What does 'a good night's sleep' mean? As you can see, The Benjamin went into considerable detail. They considered pillows, and guest rooms that started five stories above street level, and soundproof windows; luxury sheets; aromatherapy; massages; satin sleep masks; tips for "executive" naps; a menu of 11 special pillows, including the "Snore-No-More"; and special sleep-inducing foods, like banana bread with peanut butter.

And the list is only part of the 'fleshing out' of the 'a good night's sleep'. The Benjamin is focusing their entire energy on 'a good night's sleep'. So much so, that if they do a good job of propagating the uniqueness, their customers will know exactly why they choose The Benjamin, when there are scores of other hotels in New York.

But there's a downside to this uniqueness exercise.
You can clearly see how a company can stand out from its
competition. But then when you sit down to do your own
uniqueness, you end up being vague.

So how do we know if we're being vague?
I worked with a bread company. And their bread was extremely fresh

But everyone says: Our bread is fresh.

So how do you qualify freshness?
They actually never let their bread stay for more than two days on
the supermarket shelves. But the customers never did know it (they
still don't).

And so the bread brand fights against cheaper bread brands.

What's more interesting is that their bread would get mouldy in
about 4-5 days if left in moist conditions. So people would think
their bread is not good, because the other bread wouldn't get
mouldy. But the fact was that good bread does get mouldy, because
good bread has no preservatives. Crappy bread can be left out
forever, and it stays just fine. Because it's loaded with preservatives.

But what if you want to preserve bread to oven-freshness?
Put it in the freezer as fast as possible. Then simply
heat it, and it puffs back to normal freshness.

Now I could go on and on, about bread.
And you'd continue to be interested.
But this bread company didn't think a customer
would be interested.

They thought the facts were boring.

You don't think they're boring, do you?

Terms like 'fresh' or
'quality' or 'service' are
useless. How 'fresh
is fresh?' Two minute
old? Two days old? Two
weeks old? Ooh, what's
that fishy smell?

They could own the market with the word 'fresh', but they don't.
And they won't. Unless they educate their customers about what freshness means.

What does freshness mean?
What does quickest mean?
What does quality mean?
What does fun mean?
What does structure mean?

As a customer I want specifics.
The Benjamin fleshes out the detail, but most companies simply stick to something vague like 'we have the best quality. Or we have the best service'.

Ugh!

Don't be silly. Qualify your uniqueness. Flesh it out. Make it alive not just for your own business, but make it alive for your customers as well. And that's how you get a factor of uniqueness. [2]

---

[2] Uniqueness isn't just restricted to companies and businesses. You can create your own personal uniqueness too. You can decide to be the most technologically advanced person in your company. Or the most reliable. When I joined my first job at the Leo Burnett ad agency in Mumbai, India, I created my uniqueness by turning up to work before anyone else.

You see I was a rookie copywriter. I couldn't impress anyone with my writing, or my knowledge of human behaviour. So instead I just turned up earlier than everyone else. I'd show up to work at 7:00 am and study all the advertising books in the agency library. The CEO of the company used to show up at 7:30 am. And do his rounds. In less than a week, the CEO's secretary told me that the CEO wanted to know who was this person who was turning up earlier than he did. In less than a week, I stood out from well over 200 employees. In less than a month, everyone knew the nut who turned up at 7:00 am ☺.

If you were to visit my website at www.psychotactics.com, and read the 'About Us' page, you'll notice that I get to work at 4 am every day (yes, even in the winter, though admittedly it's tougher when it's freezing cold). Again, this highlights a factor of how to create personal uniqueness. The uniqueness of Psychotactics is different from my personal uniqueness. And so you need to create both: A personal as well as a company uniqueness. And if you're employed by the company, you can still create a personal uniqueness based on something you aspire to be or do in future. Yup, make it your DNA. Then propagate the uniqueness, so everyone else knows it as well.

And yes, we've taken all those seven bags off the conveyor belt. It's now time to summarise, give you some check lists and help you create your own audit.

So a check-listing we go. But first let's detour back to our two recurring examples and put the finishing touch.

Website strategy workshop

Target Profile: Howard R.
Problem: *How do I grow my internet business, without compromising on my ethics?*
Solution: *Here's how to create a website strategy that's ethical, yet extremely profitable.*

Objections:
- *Not sure if I have time to implement more information*
- *Travel always takes time and energy*
- *I've just got myself a project manager which leaves me with fewer discretionary dollars*
- *Not sure if there's an overlap of information from other courses*
- *I don't need more tactics. What I need is a strategy.*

Testimonial:
"I figured the website workshop would be a rehashing of older material."

Before the website workshop, I had my doubts about what I could learn. I have been on 5000bc for more than a year, read The Brain Audit - I'm even in the Protégé program. So I was a little skeptical about hearing anything new; I figured it'd be a rehashing of older material.

I also didn't know how I would swing the time away - I've been so busy implementing the Protégé teachings, and I was concerned that this might take me off-target.

And here's what I found:
I don't think I can really put into words how comprehensive and integrative the class was. We learned amazing material. We learned how to apply it to our businesses. We discussed and shared with others, so it wasn't just direct learning, it was tangential - we were "cross-pollinated" by everyone else's epiphanies, so the learning was exponential. It was pretty darn amazing!

Risk Reversal:
1) Money-Back Guarantee
2) Ask-Anyone Guarantee.

Uniqueness: *No information dump. It's not a blah, blah information dump. You get all the information weeks in advance, so you can assimilate the information. Then at the workshop, we work through specific concepts making it a reality.*

An allergy clinic

Target Profile: Tricia M.
Problem: *How do I get rid of my allergic reaction to wine?*
Solution: *Here's how you can get rid of the allergic reaction in less than 24 hours (and without any pills or medication whatsoever).*

Objections:
- *I've tried these anti-allergy clinics before and it didn't work for me*
- *The treatment seems to be quite expensive*
- *Will I have to go for several treatments on a recurring basis?*
- *What if the treatment doesn't work for me?*

Testimonial:
"I thought the treatment would be quite expensive. And I was right!"

The treatment was quite expensive. But was it worth the expense? Let's see. I've had this allergy for well over twelve years. And no matter what I did to get rid of the allergy, nothing seemed to work.

In fact, when I really think about it, I may have spent far more money popping some kind of anti-allergy pills that only brought me temporary relief.

And here's what I found:
The allergy clinic treatment on the other hand, worked like magic. It's been six months since I've sneezed. And I can tell you I've been enjoying my red wine. I no longer have to rush home early with my face all puffy and red-eyed. I can stay and enjoy the company of my friends. And of course, when my husband and I spend a romantic dinner, I can enjoy a glass or two of fine wine, and the evening doesn't end up with me having to drink tomato juice instead!

Risk Reversal:
1) Testimonials of clients with similar issues
2) No pills or invasive techniques guarantee.

Uniqueness: *Fixes the problem permanently within 24 hours of treatment.*

Summary: The Uniqueness

- There's a fundamental flaw in uniqueness. We're asked to slap a uniqueness onto our business. And because we simply attach a uniqueness to our business, the uniqueness appears cheesy. And forced.

- Finding a uniqueness is a pretty tough job. Clients aren't much help. Family or friends aren't much help either. And the reason why finding a uniqueness is such a tough job, is because you're trying to 'find' uniqueness.

- Instead of finding your uniqueness, it's easier (and more efficient) to create your uniqueness. To create your uniqueness, all you have to do is make a wish for your customers. If there is one thing you'd wish to improve in the life of your customers, what would that one thing be?

Problem
↓
Solution
↓
Target Profile
↓
Trigger
↓
Objections
↓
Testimonials
↓
Risk Reversal
↓
Uniqueness

- One thing. One thing. One thing. One thing. One thing. One thing. One thing. One thing. One thing. One thing. I've had to say 'One thing' ten times, just to remind you that it's easy to be tempted to choose two things. Or more. e.g. Dominos Pizza chose speed of delivery. The Benjamin chose an 'excellent night's sleep.' One thing!

- The three reasons to create uniqueness are:
  a) You can make your company's offering simple and understandable.
  b) It becomes the DNA of your company. Everything revolves around that uniqueness.
  c) Your customers and the media start to see you as different, and hence newsworthy.

- It ain't enough to simply create the uniqueness. You have to make sure that everyone knows. And the best way to test whether you've done a good job is to ask your customer if they know why you're different. And every customer should respond in a similar manner.

- Before you go out into the great wide world propagating your uniqueness, you can test it. Swap your logo with another company's logo. Does the uniqueness work for your competitor? If so, it's time to go back to the drawing board and find a new uniqueness.

- Creating a factor of uniqueness is hard work. Which is precisely why you should do the hard work. Because it's so much hard work, your competition will keep procrastinating, and give you a massive head-start, and you may also attract the competition's customers with your uniqueness.

- Create your uniqueness using three steps:
  Step 1: Make a big list of what makes your business unique;
  Step 2: Weighted ranking will help you decide on the most important reason;
  Step 3: Flesh out the uniqueness to create more clarity.

- Qualify your uniqueness. Don't just say 'fresh'. What does 'fresh' mean?

- If you remove all the bags from the conveyor belt, you can still lose your customers if you don't bring out the uniqueness of your business/product/service. You don't want to throw away all your hard work, so make sure you create your uniqueness. It's important for you and your employees to know what makes you different. It gives the company/product/service a measure of pride and distinction. And a spotlight in an increasingly noisy market.

Checklist

Covering what we've just covered!

Checklist: The Problem

List all your customers' problems.

Isolate the three main problems.

Isolate the biggest problem.

Checklist: The Solution

Isolate the solution that solves the biggest problem.

Is your 'solution statement' the mirror-image of the 'problem statement'?

Have you audited your communication to check that the solution doesn't pop up first? (It should come after the problem).

Checklist: The Target Profile

Who is your target audience? What is the demographic?

Now choose three people from that demographic as your target profiles.

Narrow it down to one person.

Speak to that person and get a list of problems (with regard to a product/service).

Choose one problem then expand it.

Use that very same person to get feedback (so be aware that what you hear and what they are saying may be different).

Checklist: The Trigger

List your target profile.

List the main problem.

List the main solution.

Now test the trigger. Do you get the response: 'What do you mean by that?' or 'How do you do that?'

If you do not get the response, you need to rework your trigger. Start from the top again.

Checklist: Biggest Objection

Brainstorm all the possible objections to your product or service.

Now list all the answers to all the objections.

List the biggest objection and the answer.

Checklist: Testimonials

Step 1: Get the Testimonials

1) What was the obstacle that would have prevented you from buying this product/service?

2) What did you find as a result of buying this product/service?

3) What specific feature did you like most about this product/service?

4) What would be three other benefits about this product/service?

5) Would you recommend this product/service? If so, why?

6) Is there any thing you'd like to add?

Checklist: Testimonials

Step 2: Link the testimonials to each objection.

Objection 1:

Testimonial:

Objection 2:

Testimonial:

Objection 3:

Testimonial:

Objection 4:

Testimonial:

Checklist: Risk Reversal

Identify the obvious risk.

Identify the hidden risk.

Decide on your risk reversal.

Name the risk reversal for your product/service.

Product/Service 1:

Risk Reversal:

Product/Service 2:

Risk Reversal:

Product/Service 3:

Risk Reversal:

Checklist: Your Uniqueness

Write down what you <u>want to do </u>in your business that's different from everyone else?

List all the factors that could make your business unique.

Use 'Weighted Ranking' to decide.

Now list only one factor that is going to be your point of uniqueness.

Flesh out the uniqueness to create more clarity.

Does your uniqueness solve a problem for a specific audience?

Test your uniqueness to see that it is really unique.

List how you are going to propagate your uniqueness.

Website:
Brochure:
Promotional Material:
Business Card:
Other:

Epilogue
The end is closer than you think

Epilogue

Epilogue is a fancy word for 'we're coming to the end'.

Because there is a starting point.
You see I wasn't always in marketing. In fact, I didn't do much marketing at all for the first 15 years of my business.

And yet my business (yes, I was a professional cartoonist) did very well. So well in fact that instead of working out of my parents' house, I had an office. And I had staff. And I'd go for long lunches and to the bowling alley in the middle of the day.

So it's quite possible to run a business with little or no marketing at all. But without marketing, there was no structure. And always a factor of uncertainty.

Some months I'd have tons of work.
Some months, I'd twiddle my thumbs.
And some months I'd decide to take a break
and go on vacation.

But it was hard to enjoy the vacation,
because it always meant that while I was
away I wasn't earning anything. And there was a pretty good chance that my clients were getting someone else to do their assignments. And that just meant more competition.

There seemed to be no way out of the trap.
If I didn't go on vacation, I'd feel jaded and my work would suffer. If I did go on vacation, I'd lose revenue and bolster the competition.

What's a cartoonist to do? The answer for me at least, lay in understanding marketing. And from that moment on, my world has never been the same. Suddenly I started to understand structure a lot better. I began to understand systems.

And even more structure.

And so I began to read more.
I started to literally read two books a week.
Over a hundred books a year. I devoured
every book on marketing, management,
spiritualism, history and biographies (I often
maxed out the library card taking home as
many as thirty books at a time).

And from that mixed reading list came The Brain Audit.

You see the route to The Brain Audit was an interesting one.
As you already know The Brain Audit didn't start out as a book. The
Brain Audit was just a speech and some notes. And I'm not even
sure it was called The Brain Audit back then.

But in my thirst for even more marketing knowledge, I got in touch
with an internet marketer. And I asked for his products in exchange
for cartoons.

Well, he was happy to barter.

And in our conversation, I mentioned about this book I'd written.
And I asked this internet marketer if he'd like to take a look at it. He
agreed to take a look at the book.

And then he did something quite interesting.

He got a whole bunch of his friends to write
up testimonials about the book. And he told
me that he was going to promote the book to
his list. All I had to do was set up an affiliate
program and get some sort of merchant
account.

And he was giving me seven days to get it all done.

I was excited and horrified.
You see my wife Renuka and I had been doing our research on merchant accounts for a good two months prior to this discussion with this internet marketer. And there we were with a deadline of just seven days.

Amazingly, we did manage to find a service called Clickbank[1] that not only accepted payments, but also had a built in affiliate program.

Then we contacted the internet marketer and waited.

A month passed. And nothing happened.

I kept in touch. He said he was busy.

A second month passed.

And still nothing.

But then an amazing thing happened.
Someone wanted to buy The Brain Audit. Someone actually found our page on the website, and wanted to buy a copy.

Except she wanted to pay by Paypal.

Ugh!

So there we were scrambling again, to put another payment system together. But once it was done, she bought the first copy. And the internet marketer was still nowhere in sight. [2]

---

[1] We no longer use Clickbank, but it was a saviour back in those early days.

[2] He never did promote our book finally. We just trundled on selling to our own list of interested customers.

And without his direct help, we'd made our first sale.
So we did a jig around the room.

Actually Renuka did.

Every time we'd make a sale, she'd do the 'Renuka dance'.

And so bolstered with this new-found success, I started speaking at small networking breakfasts. A friend mentioned that I should try and sell The Brain Audit at the events.

Of course, I wasn't so sure selling The Brain Audit was a good idea. People were coming to the event to network and have a breakfast, not to hear a sales pitch.

But he convinced me otherwise.
He told me that people who liked what I had to say, would then be keen to read more. And the book provided more. Never mind that it was just an e-book in a PDF format.

So there we were at a meeting near Lake Taupo (about 280 km/175 miles from Auckland). And there were about 40 people in the room. I stood up, and spoke about The Brain Audit. And then asked people if they'd like to buy it. And thirty people bought it right away.

What's fascinating is that they couldn't see the book.
They were literally paying for a PDF file.

And because I wasn't expecting to sell anything, I didn't even have a printout of that PDF file. So in effect the audience was buying something they couldn't see.

You have to remember this was the year 2002.
Not a lot of people were internet-savvy back then. A website was a reasonable novelty. Blogs were

definitely on the fringe. At least five of the buyers of the e-book had no email address (we had to send them a CD later).

That one speaking engagement got us a chunky $900. But more importantly, it brought confidence. Suddenly I was feeling less and less like a fraud. And more and more like celebrating with a nice Cabernet Merlot.

So Renuka and I found a cozy restaurant. We ordered a nice bottle of wine. And we clinked our glasses to the start of yet another adventure.

An adventure that had started when we first moved to New Zealand.
We'd immigrated to New Zealand from Mumbai, India, in the year 2000.

We simply packed our bags and our thriving careers and started in a place where no one knew our names. In fact we'd never been to New Zealand before we first immigrated.

We'd been as far south as Australia, and people told us New Zealand was even more laid back than Australia. They told us it rained a lot. They told us there were too many sheep and too few people.

Oh goody! That sounded just fine to our ears.
Because New Zealand gave us time to catch our breath. To slow down.

Slowing down gave us time to think.
And thinking led to a change from cartoons to marketing.
And that's why you're reading this book today.

Warm regards from 4:12 am.

Sean D'Souza
P.S. Thanks for reading this book. And yes, we'll be sure to meet
again at some speaking event, workshop or just at our favourite
Takapuna cafe.

Au revoir for now.

See you online at: www.psychotactics.com

The Next Step?

A System of Care, Protection and Guidance
As you head to the last page of this book, your brain will no doubt be abuzz with all the possibilities in marketing and business.

And you'll wonder what the next step looks like.
You'll wonder if there's a system in place to help you in case you get stuck? Is there a system to help you move ahead confidently? What if you wanted to learn skills that went beyond 'The Brain Audit'?

An education can't be just an information dump. Instead it must be a system. And it must be layered so that one layer of learning builds on top of the previous layer. It must anticipate the needs of the client well in advance.

Look around you and you'll see how disciplines such as karate and yoga are organised around a system. If you look back at school or university, you knew exactly how to move to the next step. And you knew all of this because the system was put in place—in advance. This allowed you to know that you could graduate from the very same school. Get your degree from the very same college. Become a black belt in karate under the very same teacher.

We call this system 'Care, Protection and Guidance'
Look up Webster's Dictionary and you'll find the definition of the word 'client'. It defines the word 'client' as someone you should care for; someone who comes under your protection; someone you should guide. Amazingly, the definition of 'client' is akin to the relationship between a parent and a child. As a doting parent, you care for your children; guide them in the right direction; protect them from the nutcases out there. And guess what? That's what Webster's Dictionary asks you to do: create a system of 'Care, Protection and Guidance'.

That's what we've done at Psychotactics.com
1) We've created a layered system that you can easily follow.
2) The centreline of the system has specific, predefined sequence.
3) The vertical lines of the system are add-on learning modules.
4) The system is based on 'Care, Protection and Guidance.'

To see how we've helped you look far ahead in the future, take a look at the graphic below. You'll see that the progression is not only logical, but enables you to absorb what you have learned before moving ahead. This absorption and implementation not only increases your confidence, but also your expertise factor.

To find out more about how you can learn in layers (and avoid information dumps) go to http://www.psychotactics.com/nextstep and judge for yourself.

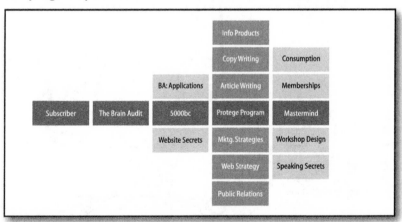

The centreline boxes represent the sequential system that enables you to move from one logical step to another. The vertical boxes represent live courses, online courses or homestudy courses or products. These courses or products are additional learning modules, once you've read 'The Brain Audit'.

Finally to get started in the crazy world of Psychotactics:
Step 1: Go to www.psychotactics.com and register for the free newsletter.
Step 2: Have a look at the sequence at www.psychotactics.com/nextstep

CPSIA information can be obtained at www.ICGtesting.com
Printed in the USA
BVOW08s2248170216

437033BV00001B/95/P